# Praise for *A Graded Reader of Biblical Hebrew*

"The ability to read, translate, interpret, and skillfully apply the Bible from the Hebrew and Greek text animates ministry and yields freshness in teaching. Students can testify that Dr. Bill Fullilove is a master teacher of the Hebrew language. This *Graded Reader*, carefully arranged and annotated, will equip students to do what they really want to do: read and use Hebrew with skill and faithfulness."
—**James L. (Jay) Harvey III**, Executive Director, Reformed Theological Seminary, New York City

"It is always right to admire the beauty of simplicity. In this *Graded Reader*, students will find biblical texts of increasing difficulty, clear and concise explanations of grammatical and syntactical concepts, and a simple format that lends itself to student learning. Rather than forcing the reader to adopt a particular syntactical methodology, Fullilove simply provides the biblical texts with footnoted helps so that students can experience the delight of reading God's Word. Many of my own students are hesitant to find the joy of learning jots and tittles from an introductory grammar, but they are always eager to read the Hebrew Bible. Fullilove's *Graded Reader* provides a superb resource for students to engage the biblical text while also having valuable references to his introductory grammar so that students can enjoy the Hebrew Bible while also solidifying their knowledge of the Hebrew language."
—**Adam J. Howell**, Assistant Professor of Old Testament Interpretation, Boyce: The College at Southern

"This *Graded Reader* is the next logical step to Fullilove's magnificent teaching grammar, moving students from their foundational deductive grasp of grammar toward more advanced inductive mastery. The texts given here are perfect for introducing students to the breadth of Biblical Hebrew, while reinforcing basic grammatical principles and challenging them to learn new ones. As in Fullilove's *Introduction*, the questions posed move beyond the typical parsing and grammatical analysis to aid students in seeing the exegetical significance of what they're learning."
—**Scott C. Jones**, Professor of Biblical and Theological Studies, Covenant College

"The *Graded Reader* offers students of Biblical Hebrew a powerful tool for retaining and improving their grasp of the language. Learning a language is more than memorization and drills, and Dr. Fullilove serves the endeavor as he guides us through representative passages from the biblical text. Thank you for this resource."
—**Scott Redd**, President and Associate Professor of Old Testament, Reformed Theological Seminary, Washington, DC

"Fullilove addresses a real gap in language learning with this *Graded Reader*. He places students at the center yet again, providing even more resources to help them in the ultimate goal of their study: learning to read Hebrew now and in the future. This resource will provide students with the much-needed encouragement to persist with their Hebrew and to consolidate their early learning."
—**C. A. Strine**, Vice-Chancellor's Fellow and Lecturer in Hebrew Bible, University of Sheffield; Author, *Sworn Enemies: The Divine Oath, the Book of Ezekiel, and the Polemics of Exile*

# Praise for *Introduction to Hebrew*

"Bill Fullilove's new grammar of Biblical Hebrew is an outstanding introduction to the language for beginning students. The author presents the basic material clearly and cogently, while deftly incorporating insights gleaned from the latest research. Beginners will enjoy starting to read actual excerpts from the Bible at an early stage; and by the end, they will be well equipped for the task of Old Testament exegesis. I warmly and enthusiastically recommend this fine new textbook."

—**Ed Cook**, Chairman, Department of Semitic and Egyptian Languages and Literatures; Associate Professor, The Catholic University of America

"From beginning to end, Fullilove keeps in mind that the ultimate goal of biblical language-learning is to grasp the message of Scripture so that the text can master us. This is an exegetically oriented beginning Hebrew grammar. It sets itself apart by teaching not only what morphology and clause syntax are but how our knowledge of Hebrew helps us understand God's Book. Fullilove gets students into the biblical text early and then uses creative paths to nurture discovery and to point forward toward application. The chapters are well structured and clear, and the overall work is highly creative. This is a guidebook that will motivate students to learn, so I joyfully recommend this grammar."

—**Jason S. DeRouchie**, Professor of Old Testament and Biblical Theology, Bethlehem College & Seminary; Coauthor, *A Modern Grammar for Biblical Hebrew*

"In my experience, students work incredibly hard to learn Hebrew. But since they don't experience firsthand the value of reading Hebrew for exegesis, a regrettable number of them don't maintain their Hebrew and therefore never get to see its payoff. *Introduction to Hebrew* by Bill Fullilove, a great new resource for Hebrew teachers and students, was designed to solve that problem. Its chief brilliance lies in showing students the value of Hebrew for exegesis from the very beginning of their study. Every chapter guides the students through an exegetical exercise based on the material just learned. (Even if all they know is the alphabet!) It teaches them to use reference tools and to draw conclusions *based on their understanding of Hebrew*. This not only shows them the value of knowing Hebrew, but trains them to use those reference tools so that they come out equipped rather than intimidated by them. Hurray!"

—**Elizabeth Groves**, Lecturer in Biblical Hebrew, Westminster Theological Seminary

"It is a joy to commend Bill Fullilove's *Introduction to Hebrew* to present and future pastors and to serious readers of the Scripture. He has found ways to make the language so accessible and yet filled with such accuracy that many who thought Hebrew was beyond their reach will find it readily and comfortably right at hand."

—**Walter C. Kaiser Jr.**, President Emeritus, Gordon-Conwell Theological Seminary

"Here's the book that I wish I had been given—and from which I wish I had been instructed—when I was a student of Hebrew. Ministry students are frankly goal-oriented when it comes to language study. We want our language knowledge to directly and continually enable us to interpret God's Word. Bill Fullilove's *Introduction to Hebrew* never loses sight of this goal. I highly recommend it."
—**Tim Keller**, Redeemer Presbyterian Church, New York City

"Dr. Bill Fullilove has successfully produced a new grammar that demonstrates the benefits of Biblical Hebrew for exegetical matters. From something as basic as the alphabet to more sophisticated linguistic concepts, he provides practical steps in gaining a knowledge of Hebrew as an essential tool to understand the message of Scripture. Diligent students will find this grammar rewarding and see immediate fruits of their labors."
—**Peter Lee**, Associate Professor of Old Testament, Reformed Theological Seminary, Washington, DC

"Many students begin their study of Biblical Hebrew with enthusiasm but lose their zeal because they see no practical benefit. Dr. Fullilove shows beginning students the value of learning Hebrew every step of the way. His approach will encourage students to keep moving forward until they master the basic grammar of Biblical Hebrew."
—**Richard L. Pratt Jr.**, President, Third Millennium Ministries

# A GRADED READER OF BIBLICAL

# HEBREW

## MASTERING DIFFERENT LITERARY STYLES FROM SIMPLE TO ADVANCED

## William Fullilove

PUBLISHING

P.O. BOX 817 • PHILLIPSBURG • NEW JERSEY 08865-0817

Unless otherwise indicated, all Scripture quotations are the author's own translation.

Scripture quotations marked as ESV are from the ESV® Bible (The Holy Bible, English Standard Version®), copyright © 2001 by Crossway, a publishing ministry of Good News Publishers. Used by permission. All rights reserved.

ISBN: 978-1-62995-648-0 (pbk)

Printed in the United States of America

To Callie and Evie, with prayers that you will grow to be an אֵשֶׁת חַיִל, just like your mother.

Additional Aids for Teachers or Students are available

at **www.introductiontohebrew.com**.

# Contents

Preface      vii

Part I: Readings in Hebrew Narrative

א      (1)      2 Samuel 9:1–13      1

ב      (2)      Genesis 50:1–14      8

ג      (3)      Genesis 50:15–26      15

ד      (4)      2 Chronicles 1:1–18      20

ה      (5)      Nehemiah 1:1–11      29

Part II: Readings in Legal Texts

ו      (6)      Leviticus 1:1–17      39

ז      (7)      Deuteronomy 22:1–12      46

ח      (8)      Deuteronomy 24:1–18      52

Part III: Readings in the Psalms

ט      (9)      Psalms 23, 24, and 100      63

י      (10)      Psalm 19      72

Part IV: Readings in Prophetic Literature

יא      (11)      Micah 6:1–8, Amos 2:1–5      79

יב      (12)      Isaiah 52:13–53:12      85

Part V: Readings in Wisdom Literature

יג      (13)      Proverbs 28:1–16      95

יד      (14)      Job 28:1–28      99

# Preface

The way you learn Hebrew is NOT the way to retain it!  In learning a language, there is an inevitable need for memorization, vocabulary drills, paradigms, etc.  Further, there is a need for continuous review.  At the same time, however, you will not ultimately retain any language by doing vocabulary cards and reciting paradigms.  In the end, you retain a language by using it, by reading and speaking it.  This graded reader seeks to bridge the gap between the initial learning stage and that ongoing use of the language.  It attempts to address several challenges:

First, at the end of any introductory grammar, a student has not yet really "learned" the language.  Better put, you have been exposed to all of the necessary concepts, but even the best students need to transition from a structured deductive pedagogy to a more inductive pedagogy.  You may have been taught the difference between a vocal and a silent shewa or the different possible uses of an infinitive construct, but the way that knowledge will start to "stick" is when you see those features in their natural environment, by reading continuous texts.  This graded reader is therefore keyed to my earlier volume *Introduction to Hebrew: A Guide for Learning and Using Biblical Hebrew*, referencing you back to the introductory grammar in order to facilitate review of all you have learned.  (Any time you see the note "See section . . ." without any other modifiers, that is a reference back to *Introduction to Hebrew*.)  In that inductive review your knowledge will really start to be cemented.

Second, the student who launches from his or her introductory grammar into the Hebrew Bible is often knocked backward by the variety of texts and by the different characteristics of those texts.  Most students are decently well prepared to read simple narratives but are bewildered when they turn to books like Job or Proverbs.  The graded reader approach again bridges the gap, starting with texts for which you are well prepared and then moving to progressively more difficult texts as your experience and skills grow.  The passages begin with prose and then progressively move into more challenging pieces of poetry, at the same time surveying various genres of Biblical Hebrew.

Third, to really use Hebrew well in understanding and teaching texts, an introductory grammar is just that – an introduction.  If you want to use your Hebrew well and to become a student of the text, you need to begin to use more robust reference tools.  You must eventually move beyond simply flipping back through your introductory textbook and searching for what it said on a given topic.  *Introduction to Hebrew* already began introducing you to more robust research tools such as lexical aids.  To further that goal, this graded reader regularly references *An Introduction to Biblical Hebrew Syntax (IBHS),* by Bruce Waltke and Michael Patrick

O'Connor, one of the standard reference works in the field, a work that will fill in the gaps that are of necessity present in an introductory grammar. I was privileged to study under both of these men, each of whom worked to demonstrate, encourage, and inspire excellence in the study of Hebrew.

Given the nature of the task, this graded reader is presented in a workbook format. While it is best used along with a copy of *Introduction to Hebrew*, its predecessor volume, it can be used profitably to follow on any other introductory grammar as well. Likewise, this graded reader can be used successfully with a small lexicon, such as Holliday's *A Concise Hebrew and Aramaic Lexicon of the Old Testament*, but access to a research lexicon such as Koehler and Baumgartner's *Hebrew and Aramaic Lexicon of the Old Testament (HALOT)*, of which Holladay's work is a very helpful abridgment, will give the greatest value.

Thanks are again due to the good men and women at P&R Publishing who believed in the first volume and now in this one. Thanks are also deeply due to my wife and daughters, who put up with this habit of writing books. And, in the end, all thanks are due to God for his grace.

Read and learn and enjoy!

SDG

William Fullilove

August 2018

# PART I

## Readings in Hebrew Narrative

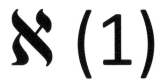 **א (1)**

2 Samuel 9 provides the first of two examples of what has traditionally been called "Classical Biblical Hebrew" (CBH), the relatively unified style of Biblical Hebrew that is seen from Genesis all the way through 2 Kings. Classical Biblical Hebrew is, by and large, the grammatical structure that you have learned through *Introduction to Hebrew*, and these two exercises give you practice in applying the skills you have learned to complete narrative texts.

1     וַיֹּאמֶר דָּוִד הֲכִי¹ יֶשׁ־עוֹד אֲשֶׁר נוֹתַר² לְבֵית שָׁאוּל וְאֶעֱשֶׂה³ עִמּוֹ חֶסֶד⁴

בַּעֲבוּר יְהוֹנָתָן׃

---

¹ Note that this ה is not the definite article, as the following consonant is not doubled. What function of ה is this? (See section 8.7 in *Introduction to Hebrew*.)

² Remember that I-י verbs were originally I-ו and that the ו reappears when "trapped" by a prefix. What is the root and what is the parsing of this verb? (See section 27.2.)

³ Note that this is not technically a secondary volitive in the sense defined in section 25.7, but it functions in the same way.

⁴ This word of all Hebrew nouns requires a word study to fully understand its semantic range and meaning in context. How would you gloss the word in your translation and why? (See sections 5.7 and 6.7.)

2    וּלְבֵית֩⁵ שָׁא֨וּל עֶ֜בֶד וּשְׁמ֤וֹ צִיבָא֙ וַיִּקְרְאוּ⁻לוֹ֙⁶ אֶל⁻דָּוִ֔ד⁷ וַיֹּ֖אמֶר הַמֶּ֑לֶךְ

אֵלָֽיו

הַאַתָּ֣ה צִיבָ֑א וַיֹּ֖אמֶר עַבְדֶּֽךָ׃

3    וַיֹּ֣אמֶר הַמֶּ֗לֶךְ הַאֶ֨פֶס ע֥וֹד אִישׁ֙ לְבֵ֣ית שָׁא֔וּל וְאֶעֱשֶׂ֥ה עִמּ֖וֹ חֶ֣סֶד אֱלֹהִ֑ים

---

⁵ What use of lamed is this? Consult section 11.5. The particle of existence is not always necessary when expressing possession.

⁶ Parse this verb. This is a use of the 3mp as an impersonal construction. You could translate "they called . . . ," but the "they" is an unknown entity, so the English translation can also be an impersonal passive "he was called . . ."

⁷ Note the לְ following the verb, which marks its object. Consult your lexicon to understand which gloss of the root קרא is appropriate with לְ. The preposition provides a piece of surrounding context, which is one way to distinguish the correct portion of the semantic range to use when glossing a word in your translation. (See section 6.7.)

וַיֹּ֤אמֶר צִיבָא֙ אֶל־הַמֶּ֔לֶךְ ע֛וֹד בֵּ֥ן לִיהוֹנָתָ֖ן נְכֵ֥ה רַגְלָֽיִם׃

4   וַיֹּֽאמֶר־ל֥וֹ הַמֶּ֖לֶךְ אֵיפֹ֣ה ה֑וּא וַיֹּ֤אמֶר צִיבָא֙ אֶל־הַמֶּ֔לֶךְ הִנֵּה־ה֗וּא בֵּ֚ית

מָכִ֥יר בֶּן־עַמִּיאֵ֖ל בְּל֥וֹ דְבָֽר׃[8]

5   וַיִּשְׁלַ֖ח הַמֶּ֣לֶךְ דָּוִ֑ד וַיִּקָּחֵ֕הוּ[9] מִבֵּ֛ית מָכִ֥יר בֶּן־עַמִּיאֵ֖ל מִלּ֥וֹ דְבָֽר׃

---

[8] לוֹ דְבָר is treated rightly as a place name in translations, but also note its meaning. What does that indicate about how far Mephibosheth's status has declined due to the fall of the house of Saul?

[9] If you have trouble parsing this word, note that it has a possessive suffix and also note the dagesh in the ק. (See sections 5.1 and 21.4.) The form here is clearly narrative, not a volitive, but it shares the suffixes because it is a "short form."

6   וַיָּבֹא מְפִיבֹשֶׁת בֶּן־יְהוֹנָתָן בֶּן־שָׁאוּל[10] אֶל־דָּוִד וַיִּפֹּל עַל־פָּנָיו וַיִּשְׁתָּחוּ[11]

וַיֹּאמֶר דָּוִד מְפִיבֹשֶׁת וַיֹּאמֶר הִנֵּה[12] עַבְדֶּךָ׃

7   וַיֹּאמֶר לוֹ דָוִד אַל־תִּירָא[13] כִּי עָשֹׂה[14] אֶעֱשֶׂה עִמְּךָ חֶסֶד בַּעֲבוּר יְהוֹנָתָן

אָבִיךָ וַהֲשִׁבֹתִי[15] לְךָ אֶת־כָּל־שְׂדֵה שָׁאוּל אָבִיךָ[16] וְאַתָּה תֹּאכַל לֶחֶם עַל־

---

[10] Why does the text give both the father and grandfather of Mephibosheth? How does that make sense of his following action?

[11] See section 24.6.

[12] This is a common use of הִנֵּה to indicate one's response to being summoned. (See section 8.4.)

[13] The way in which this verb is negated informs your parsing. How must this verb be parsed, given the negative particle that precedes it? (See sections 7.5 and 7.8.)

[14] What use of the infinitive absolute is this? (See section 13.1.)

[15] Do not be misled into thinking this is a narrative form by the vowel under the ו. The vowel is on account of the following guttural consonant.

[16] Saul is obviously Mephibosheth's grandfather (see verse 6). The word אָב can be used for relationships beyond that of simply the biological father.

שְׁלָחַנִי תָּמִיד:

8    וַיִּשְׁתַּ֫חוּ וַיֹּאמֶר מֶה עַבְדֶּךָ כִּי[17] פָנִ֫יתָ[18] אֶל־הַכֶּ֫לֶב הַמֵּת אֲשֶׁר כָּמֹ֫ונִי:

9    וַיִּקְרָא הַמֶּ֫לֶךְ אֶל־צִיבָא נַ֫עַר שָׁאוּל וַיֹּ֫אמֶר אֵלָיו כֹּל אֲשֶׁר הָיָה לְשָׁאוּל

וּלְכָל־בֵּיתֹו נָתַ֫תִּי[19] לְבֶן־אֲדֹנֶ֫יךָ:

---

[17] Which use of כִּי is this? (See section 14.10.)

[18] Use your lexicon to determine the best gloss for פנה when used with the preposition אֶל. (See section 6.7.)

[19] None of the translation options you learned for the perfect in section 3.7 are quite correct here. Remember that an introductory grammar only gives you the most common possibilities for the translation of a Hebrew verbal form. Consult *IBHS* section 30.5.1.d for the best translation value for this Hebrew perfect.

10  וְעָבַדְתָּ[20] לּוֹ אֶת־הָאֲדָמָה אַתָּה וּבָנֶיךָ וַעֲבָדֶיךָ וְהֵבֵאתָ וְהָיָה לְבֶן־אֲדֹנֶיךָ

לֶחֶם וַאֲכָלוֹ וּמְפִיבֹשֶׁת בֶּן־אֲדֹנֶיךָ יֹאכַל[21] תָּמִיד לֶחֶם עַל־שֻׁלְחָנִי

וּלְצִיבָא חֲמִשָּׁה עָשָׂר בָּנִים וְעֶשְׂרִים עֲבָדִים:

11  וַיֹּאמֶר צִיבָא אֶל־הַמֶּלֶךְ כְּכֹל אֲשֶׁר יְצַוֶּה[22] אֲדֹנִי הַמֶּלֶךְ אֶת־עַבְדּוֹ כֵּן

יַעֲשֶׂה עַבְדֶּךָ וּמְפִיבֹשֶׁת[23] אֹכֵל עַל־שֻׁלְחָנִי[24] כְּאַחַד מִבְּנֵי הַמֶּלֶךְ:

---

[20] Note that the following string of converted perfects all take their sense from the preceding verb נָתַתִּי. How would you therefore translate them?  (See section 12.3.)

[21] This verb now breaks the series of converted perfects and therefore needs to have its modality determined by context.  How is it parsed, and how should it be translated?  (See section 5.2.)

[22] Remember that when a ו has a vowel point other than ḥolem or shureq, it must be a consonantal ו.  What is the root of this verb?

[23] Note the change in word order here.  What is implied?  (See section 15.8.)

[24] Be careful not to translate the way you *think* this should read!  What does the Hebrew text actually say? Consult the BHS text critical note to understand why translations typically say "his table" or "David's table." (See section 2.11.)

12  וְלִמְפִיבֹ֨שֶׁת֙ בֵּ֣ן קָטָ֔ן וּשְׁמֹ֖ו מִיכָ֑א וְכֹל֙ מֹושַׁ֣ב בֵּֽית־צִיבָ֔א עֲבָדִ֖ים

לִמְפִיבֹֽשֶׁת׃

13  וּמְפִיבֹ֗שֶׁת יֹשֵׁב֙ בִּיר֣וּשָׁלִַ֔ם כִּ֞י<sup>25</sup> עַל־שֻׁלְחַ֤ן הַמֶּ֙לֶךְ֙ תָּמִ֔יד ה֖וּא אֹכֵ֑ל<sup>26</sup> וְה֥וּא

פִּסֵּ֖חַ שְׁתֵּ֥י רַגְלָֽיו׃ פ<sup>27</sup>

---

<sup>25</sup> Which use of כִּי is this?  (See section 14.10.)

<sup>26</sup> Is this a descriptive or identifying clause?  How do you know?  (See section 15.8.)

<sup>27</sup> This letter stands for *petuḥa*, the end of a segment in an ancient reading tradition of the Hebrew Bible.

Genesis 50 (covered in this chapter and the next), the end of the Joseph narrative, gives a second example of Classical Biblical Hebrew prose.  The first fourteen verses also contain two relatively simple text critical decisions which will give you practice in thinking through text critical questions.

1    וַיִּפֹּל יוֹסֵף עַל־פְּנֵי אָבִיו וַיֵּבְךְּ עָלָיו וַיִּשַּׁק־לֽוֹ:[1]

2    וַיְצַו יוֹסֵף אֶת־עֲבָדָיו אֶת־הָרֹפְאִים[2] לַחֲנֹט אֶת־אָבִיו וַיַּחַנְטוּ הָרֹפְאִים

אֶת־יִשְׂרָאֵֽל:[3]

---

[1] See sections 10.4 and 11.3 for the form of אָב before this possessive suffix.

[2] Note how both nouns are marked by the definite direct object marker.  This is the grammatical phenomenon known as "apposition," where two nouns are used to mutually describe each other.  If the conjunction ־וּ were used, these two nouns might be considered separate groups, but with apposition, this is one group described with two terms.

[3] Note the name used for Jacob in verse 2.  Name changes in the Bible are almost always significant to the characterization of the passage.  Review the Jacob narrative and when the names "Jacob" and "Israel" are used for him.  Compare this to the Abraham narrative and when the names "Abram" and "Abraham" are used.  What is the significance of using the name "Israel" here?

3 וַיִּמְלְאוּ־לוֹ אַרְבָּעִים יוֹם כִּי⁴ כֵּן יִמְלְאוּ יְמֵי הַחֲנֻטִים⁵ וַיִּבְכּוּ אֹתוֹ מִצְרַיִם

שִׁבְעִים יוֹם:

4 וַיַּעַבְרוּ יְמֵי בְכִיתוֹ⁶ וַיְדַבֵּר יוֹסֵף אֶל־בֵּית פַּרְעֹה לֵאמֹר⁷ אִם־נָא⁸ מָצָאתִי

חֵן בְּעֵינֵיכֶם דַּבְּרוּ־נָא בְּאָזְנֵי⁹ פַרְעֹה לֵאמֹר:

---

⁴ What use of כִּי is this?  (See section 14.10.)

⁵ This is a nominal/adjectival form, but it clearly relates to the previous verb חנט. What verbal form would it be if it were parsed as a verb?

⁶ This is a noun form from the verbal root בכה in the previous verse.

⁷ It is a choice of English style as to whether this infinitive construct should be translated or should be replaced with English quotation marks.  What is the verbal root?

⁸ Note that Joseph is obviously being polite in his speech; however, the particle נָא is not part of that politeness.  What role does it play?  (See section 8.8.)

⁹ The vowel under the א is a qameṣ ḥatup. How do you know?  (See section 2.5.)  Pronouncing the word correctly should help you recognize this vocabulary word.

5   אָבִי[10] הִשְׁבִּיעַנִי[11] לֵאמֹר הִנֵּה אָנֹכִי מֵת[12] בְּקִבְרִי[13] אֲשֶׁר כָּרִיתִי לִי בְּאֶרֶץ

כְּנַעַן שָׁמָּה[14] תִּקְבְּרֵנִי וְעַתָּה אֶעֱלֶה־נָּא[15] וְאֶקְבְּרָה[16] אֶת־אָבִי[17] וְאָשׁוּבָה[18]׃

6   וַיֹּאמֶר פַּרְעֹה עֲלֵה וּקְבֹר[19] אֶת־אָבִיךָ כַּאֲשֶׁר הִשְׁבִּיעֶךָ׃

---

[10] Note that this is a quotation, so the word order rules of Hebrew narrative (see sections 12.4 and 15.8) do not apply. Embedded speech is, as far as the narrative itself is considered, a sequential act, so the analysis of the word order in this narrative is governed by וַיְדַבֵּר in verse 4.

[11] Consider the text critical note on this word. Several witnesses have two additional words. Which witnesses and what additional words do they suggest? Do you believe those additional words are likely authentic, or is the Masoretic Text a preferable reading? Why?

[12] Parse this verbal form. Which use of the participle is it? How do you know? (Consult *IBHS* section 37.6.)

[13] Within the quotation that comprises most of verse 5 (but not in the overall narrative–see note 9) there is significance to Jacob placing this prepositional phrase well before the verb that governs it. What is that significance?

[14] What is the function of the ה attached to שָׁם in this verse? (See section 8.9.)

[15] What modality should be used to translate this imperfect? Why? (See section 5.2.)

[16] Parse this verb. How should it be translated? (See section 25.7.)

[17] Consider the text critical note on this word. One witness has two additional words. Which witness and what additional words does it suggest? Do you believe those additional words are likely authentic, or is the Masoretic Text a preferable reading? Why?

[18] The ה on the end of this verb makes the parsing unambiguous. What is the correct parsing? (See section 7.2.)

[19] Parse this verb. How should it be translated? (See section 25.7.)

7     וַיַּ֥עַל יוֹסֵ֖ף לִקְבֹּ֣ר אֶת־אָבִ֑יו וַיַּֽעֲל֨וּ אִתּ֜וֹ כָּל־עַבְדֵ֤י פַרְעֹה֙ זִקְנֵ֣י[20] בֵית֔וֹ וְכֹ֖ל

זִקְנֵ֥י אֶֽרֶץ־מִצְרָֽיִם:[21]

8     וְכֹל֙ בֵּ֣ית יוֹסֵ֔ף וְאֶחָ֖יו[22] וּבֵ֣ית אָבִ֑יו רַ֗ק טַפָּם֙[23] וְצֹאנָ֣ם וּבְקָרָ֔ם עָזְב֖וּ[24]

בְּאֶ֥רֶץ גֹּֽשֶׁן:

---

[20] This is an adjective serving a nominal function in construct. How should it be translated?

[21] What does this indicate about the text's portrayal of the honor given to Joseph?

[22] Is this a singular or plural noun? How do you know? (See section 11.3.)

[23] Consult the lexical resources available to you (see sections 5.7 and 6.7) and determine the types of people included in this noun. Why do you choose the answer you do?

[24] Of the various glosses of the Qal form of this verb available to you in your lexicon, which fits best in this context? Why?

9    וַיַּ֣עַל עִמּ֔וֹ גַּם־רֶ֖כֶב גַּם־פָּרָשִׁ֑ים וַיְהִ֥י הַֽמַּחֲנֶ֖ה כָּבֵ֥ד[25] מְאֹֽד[26]׃

10    וַיָּבֹ֜אוּ עַד־גֹּ֣רֶן הָאָטָ֗ד[27] אֲשֶׁר֙ בְּעֵ֣בֶר הַיַּרְדֵּ֔ן וַיִּ֨סְפְּדוּ־[28]שָׁ֔ם מִסְפֵּ֛ד גָּד֥וֹל

וְכָבֵ֖ד מְאֹ֑ד וַיַּ֧עַשׂ לְאָבִ֛יו אֵ֖בֶל שִׁבְעַ֥ת יָמִֽים׃

11    וַיַּ֡רְא יוֹשֵׁב֩[29] הָאָ֨רֶץ הַֽכְּנַעֲנִ֜י אֶת־הָאֵ֗בֶל[30] בְּגֹ֙רֶן֙ הָֽאָטָ֔ד וַיֹּ֣אמְר֔וּ אֵֽבֶל־כָּבֵ֥ד

---

[25] Note that the verb is singular, but the following compound subject has a singular and a plural element. This use of a singular verb for a plural subject is relatively common when the subject being referenced is acting as a unity.

[26] Of the glosses for כָּבֵד available to you in your lexical resources, which one would you choose here? Why?

[27] This word is typically glossed on its own in the lexica but also often under the entry for גֹּרֶן.

[28] Note that the third letter of this root is ד, not ר!

[29] If you have difficulty parsing this word, try writing it without the *mater* to make the form more recognizable. Remember that *matres* do not impact either the parsing or the meaning of a word; they are merely a different way of writing the same word. (See section 2.6.)

[30] Note that the first use of this word (in verse 10) did not have a definite article. That was a "first mention" use of a word, and as new information to the reader, it is typically not marked with the definite article. The definite article on this "second use" of the word indicates to you as a reader that you should be able to identify the specific אֵבֶל that is referenced in this verse.

זֶה לְמִצְרַ֫יִם עַל־כֵּ֖ן קָרָ֣א[31] שְׁמָהּ֙[32] אָבֵ֣ל מִצְרַ֔יִם אֲשֶׁ֖ר בְּעֵ֥בֶר הַיַּרְדֵּֽן׃

12 וַיַּעֲשׂ֥וּ בָנָ֖יו ל֑וֹ כֵּ֖ן כַּאֲשֶׁ֥ר צִוָּֽם[33]׃

13 וַיִּשְׂא֨וּ אֹת֤וֹ בָנָיו֙ אַ֔רְצָה[34] כְּנַ֔עַן וַיִּקְבְּר֣וּ אֹת֔וֹ בִּמְעָרַ֖ת שְׂדֵ֥ה הַמַּכְפֵּלָ֑ה[35]

אֲשֶׁ֣ר קָנָ֣ה אַבְרָהָ֡ם אֶת־הַשָּׂדֶ֜ה לַאֲחֻזַּת־[36]קֶ֗בֶר מֵאֵ֛ת[37] עֶפְרֹ֥ן הַחִתִּ֖י עַל־

---

[31] Note that this verb form is singular indefinite, translated into English with the subject "one." More smooth English syntax often translates this indefinite subject with a passive verbal form–e.g., "Its name is called . . ."

[32] The Masoretic dot in the ה (called a *mappiq*–see section 2.6) indicates that this letter is to be pronounced as a consonant, even though it is in a position where it would typically be a *mater*. Assuming the Masoretes are correct in this pointing, how do you therefore analyze this ה?

[33] Note that the ם is an object suffix, not a verbal root letter.

[34] Recognizing the function of this ה will smooth your translation. What type of ה is it?

[35] This is a construct phrase with two construct forms followed by an absolute form. What type of genitive construction is this? (See *IBHS* section 9.5.2.)

[36] Of the two possible glosses for אֲחֻזָּה, which is more appropriate in this context? Why?

[37] Note that this is a compound word. What two Hebrew words comprise this form?

פְּנֵי מַמְרֵא:[38]

14    וַיָּ֣שָׁב[39] יוֹסֵ֤ף מִצְרַ֙יְמָה֙ ה֣וּא וְאֶחָ֔יו וְכָל־הָעֹלִ֥ים אִתּ֖וֹ לִקְבֹּ֣ר אֶת־אָבִ֑יו

אַחֲרֵ֖י קָבְר֥וֹ[40] אֶת־אָבִֽיו:[41]

---

[38] These last three words are sometimes translated "to the east of Mamre." and sometimes translated "near Mamre." Why?

[39] Note the singular verb with the compound subject. What does this indicate about the focus of the passage?

[40] Look carefully at the first vowel. Is it a *qameṣ* or a *qameṣ ḥatup̄*? (See section 2.5.) How do you know? How does that help you in parsing the form? (See section 13.3.)

[41] Check the text critical note at the end of this verse. Certain words are not in the Septuagint tradition. Which words? The BHS editor asks "delete?" Would you argue these words are more likely a secondary addition, and therefore to be removed, or more likely original? Why?

Chapter 3 continues the translation of Genesis 50, the end of the Joseph narrative, completing this second example of Classical Biblical Hebrew prose. It contains several additional simple text critical decisions which will continue your practice in thinking through text critical questions. The notes will now also begin to more regularly reference *IBHS* to increase your skill in working with an intermediate syntax as a reference work.

15 וַיִּרְא֤וּ אֲחֵֽי־יוֹסֵף֙ כִּי־מֵ֣ת אֲבִיהֶ֔ם וַיֹּ֣אמְר֔וּ ל֚וּ[1] יִשְׂטְמֵ֣נוּ יוֹסֵ֔ף וְהָשֵׁ֤ב יָשִׁיב֙

לָ֕נוּ אֵ֚ת כָּל־הָ֣רָעָ֔ה אֲשֶׁ֥ר גָּמַ֖לְנוּ[2] אֹתֽוֹ׃

16 וַיְצַוּ֕וּ[3] אֶל־יוֹסֵ֖ף לֵאמֹ֑ר אָבִ֣יךָ צִוָּ֔ה לִפְנֵ֥י מוֹת֖וֹ לֵאמֹֽר׃

---

[1] Consult your lexicon. How is ל֚וּ typically glossed when followed by an imperfect? How could this use of the term have developed from the typical use? How does this choice of translation relate to the modality you choose in translating the following verb?

[2] Why might the brothers have used the verb גמל here instead of the verb עשה?

[3] Note the word choice here. Why is a form of צוה used? What does it imply about the brothers' attempt to influence Joseph as they try to ensure their own safety? Check the text critical note on this word. What does

17  כֹּה־תֹאמְר֣וּ⁴ לְיוֹסֵ֗ף אָ֣נָּא שָׂ֤א⁵ נָ֨א פֶּ֤שַׁע אַחֶ֨יךָ֙ וְחַטָּאתָם֙ כִּי־⁶רָעָ֣ה גְמָל֔וּךָ

וְעַתָּ֗ה שָׂ֤א נָא֙ לְפֶ֣שַׁע עַבְדֵ֔י אֱלֹהֵ֣י אָבִ֑יךָ וַיֵּ֥בְךְּ יוֹסֵ֖ף בְּדַבְּרָ֥ם⁷ אֵלָֽיו׃

18  וַיֵּלְכוּ֙ גַּם־אֶחָ֔יו וַֽיִּפְּל֖וּ לְפָנָ֑יו וַיֹּ֣אמְר֔וּ הִנֶּ֥נּֽוּ לְךָ֖⁸ לַעֲבָדִֽים׃

19  וַיֹּ֧אמֶר אֲלֵהֶ֛ם יוֹסֵ֖ף אַל־תִּירָ֑אוּ⁹ כִּ֛י הֲתַ֥חַת¹⁰ אֱלֹהִ֖ים אָֽנִי׃

---

the Septuagint read for this verb?  What Hebrew verb would correspond to that reading?  Which verb should be preferred as the more likely original reading?  Why?

⁴ What modality should be used to translate this imperfect?  Why?  (See section 5.2.)

⁵ This is an imperative form of the root נשא.  Consult a lexicon–which gloss for the root is appropriate when used with פֶּשַׁע?  Why?

⁶ What use of כִּי is this?  (See section 14.10.)

⁷ What sense of the preposition בְּ is used here?  (See *IBHS* section 11.2.5.)

⁸ What sense of the preposition לְ is used here?  (See *IBHS* section 11.2.10.)

⁹ What type of negation is this?  Given the type of negation, how must the verb be parsed?  (See sections 7.5 and 7.8.)  Why does this type of negation fit in the current narrative?

¹⁰ What is the function of the initial הַ on this word?

16

20 וְאַתֶּ֕ם חֲשַׁבְתֶּ֥ם עָלַי֖[11] רָעָ֑ה אֱלֹהִים֙[12] חֲשָׁבָ֣הּ לְטֹבָ֔ה[13] לְמַ֗עַן עֲשֹׂ֛ה כַּיּ֥וֹם

הַזֶּ֖ה לְהַחֲיֹ֥ת עַם־רָֽב׃

21 וְעַתָּה֙ אַל־תִּירָ֔אוּ אָנֹכִ֛י אֲכַלְכֵּ֥ל[14] אֶתְכֶ֖ם וְאֶֽת־טַפְּכֶ֑ם וַיְנַחֵ֣ם אוֹתָ֔ם וַיְדַבֵּ֖ר

עַל־לִבָּֽם׃[15]

---

[11] Consult a lexicon–what gloss for חָשַׁב is most appropriate when used with the preposition עַל?

[12] The NIV, ESV, KJV, and other translations all read "but God . . ." Check the text critical note. Why do these translations likely feel it appropriate to include the conjunction "but" in the English rendering of this verse?

[13] Note the different preposition to mark the object of the same verb (חָשַׁב). How does that impact your translation?

[14] For the parsing of this verb, see section 28.6. This is typically considered a Pilpel form of the root כּוּל. As with many of the minor stems, it seems to occur because a middle-weak root is being used in the D (doubling) stem.

[15] עַל־לִבָּם is idiomatic. How would you give a dynamic equivalent translation for this term? (See section 21.7.)

17

22 וַיֵּ֤שֶׁב[16] יוֹסֵף֙ בְּמִצְרַ֔יִם ה֖וּא וּבֵ֣ית אָבִ֑יו וַיְחִ֣י יוֹסֵ֔ף מֵאָ֖ה וָעֶ֥שֶׂר שָׁנִֽים׃

23 וַיַּ֤רְא יוֹסֵף֙ לְאֶפְרַ֔יִם בְּנֵ֖י[17] שִׁלֵּשִׁ֑ים[18] גַּ֗ם בְּנֵ֤י מָכִיר֙ בֶּן־מְנַשֶּׁ֔ה יֻלְּד֖וּ[19] עַל־

בִּרְכֵּ֥י[20] יוֹסֵֽף׃

24 וַיֹּ֤אמֶר יוֹסֵף֙ אֶל־אֶחָ֔יו אָנֹכִ֖י מֵ֑ת וֵֽאלֹהִ֞ים פָּקֹ֧ד[21] יִפְקֹ֣ד אֶתְכֶ֗ם וְהֶעֱלָ֤ה

---

[16] Note again the singular verb with the compound subject. What does this say about the focus of this passage?

[17] Check the text critical note. What difference do the Samaritan Pentateuch and many of the versions show on this word? Which do you believe is more likely authentic and why?

[18] The form comes from a numeral. What does it mean in context? Consult a lexicon if necessary.

[19] As pointed, how would you parse this form? What *binyan* is more likely? (See section 17.8.)

[20] Check the text critical note. What reading does the Samaritan Pentateuch have for this word? Which do you believe is more likely authentic and why?

[21] What use of the infinitive absolute is this? (See section 13.1.)

אֶתְכֶם֙ מִן־הָאָ֣רֶץ הַזֹּ֔את אֶל־הָאָ֕רֶץ אֲשֶׁ֥ר נִשְׁבַּ֛ע לְאַבְרָהָ֥ם לְיִצְחָ֖ק

וּֽלְיַעֲקֹֽב׃

25 וַיַּשְׁבַּ֣ע יוֹסֵ֔ף אֶת־בְּנֵ֥י יִשְׂרָאֵ֖ל לֵאמֹ֑ר פָּקֹ֨ד יִפְקֹ֤ד אֱלֹהִים֙ אֶתְכֶ֔ם וְהַעֲלִתֶ֥ם

אֶת־עַצְמֹתַ֖י מִזֶּֽה׃

26 וַיָּ֣מָת יוֹסֵ֔ף בֶּן־מֵאָ֥ה וָעֶ֖שֶׂר שָׁנִ֑ים וַיַּחַנְט֣וּ אֹת֔וֹ וַיִּ֥ישֶׂם[22] בָּאָר֖וֹן[23] בְּמִצְרָֽיִם׃

---

[22] Check the text critical note. Based on the Samaritan Pentateuch, what reading does the BHS editor suggest? How would that reading be parsed? If the Samaritan Pentateuch is a better reading, what text critical error could have produced the Masoretic Text? Which reading do you think is more likely original and why?
[23] What is the semantic range of this word? Which portion of that range is intended here? How do you know? (See sections 5.7 and 6.7.)

2 Chronicles 1 is a third example of Biblical Hebrew narrative.  Unlike the first two exercises, however, 2 Chronicles 1 is an example of what has traditionally been called "Late Biblical Hebrew" (LBH).  LBH is Biblical Hebrew from after the Babylonian exile, and various factors–language contact due to world and national events, inevitable language drift, and others–mean that LBH at times shows a different set of linguistic behaviors.  This exercise helps you notice the different language expectations you should bring to an LBH text.

1  וַיִּתְחַזֵּק שְׁלֹמֹה בֶן־דָּוִיד עַל־מַלְכוּתוֹ[1] וַיהוָה אֱלֹהָיו עִמּוֹ[2] וַיְגַדְּלֵהוּ

לְמָעְלָה:[3]

2  וַיֹּאמֶר שְׁלֹמֹה לְכָל־יִשְׂרָאֵל לְשָׂרֵי הָאֲלָפִים וְהַמֵּאוֹת וְלַשֹּׁפְטִים וּלְכֹל

---

[1] Consult the lexical entry for this word in a research lexicon.  According to the beginning of the entry, it is a loanword from what language?  Loanwords from this language are a feature of LBH.  What word would this be in CBH?

[2] Note the word order for this clause.  What type of clause is it?  (See section 15.8.)

[3] This form is composed of a preposition, a substantive, and a directional ה.  Look it up in your lexicon under the entry for the noun.  This is an LBH meaning to an older construction, now functioning as an adverb of degree, glossed as "very" or "exceedingly" in this context.

נָשִׂ֥יא לְכָל־יִשְׂרָאֵ֖ל רָאשֵׁ֥י הָאָבֽוֹת:⁴

3    וַיֵּלְכ֣וּ שְׁלֹמֹ֗ה וְכָל־הַקָּהָל֙ עִמּ֔וֹ לַבָּמָ֖ה אֲשֶׁ֣ר בְּגִבְע֑וֹן כִּי־שָׁ֣ם הָיָ֗ה אֹ֣הֶל

מוֹעֵ֣ד הָֽאֱלֹהִ֔ים אֲשֶׁ֥ר עָשָׂ֛ה⁵ מֹשֶׁ֥ה עֶֽבֶד־יְהוָ֖ה בַּמִּדְבָּֽר:

4    אֲבָ֗ל⁶ אֲר֤וֹן הָֽאֱלֹהִים֙ הֶעֱלָ֤ה דָוִיד֙ מִקִּרְיַ֣ת יְעָרִ֔ים בַּהֵכִ֥ין⁷ ל֖וֹ דָּוִ֑יד כִּ֠י

---

⁴ Consult major English translations.  What word do they add in English to make sense of this construct phrase?  The phrase here seems to be an abbreviation of "household unit," a division of the nation related to the oldest living ancestor.

⁵ Given that this is past tense narration, what translational value best fits this perfect verbal form?  (See section 3.7.)

⁶ Look up this word in your lexicon.  Notice how gloss 1 is for earlier books whereas gloss 2 is marked for "later books."  CBH and LBH will at times have different glosses for the same word, as the semantic range of words can change over time.  (See section 5.7.)  Here it introduces verse 4 as a parenthetical remark that gives background to the narrative.  What would mark a circumstantial clause in CBH?  (See section 15.8.)  The asyndetic (without a conjunction) circumstantial clause is a feature of LBH.

⁷ This is the preposition בּ attached to a verbal form.  Note the vowel under the בּ.  What does this vowel imply about the Masoretes' understanding of this form?  (See section 6.4.)  Parse the verbal form and translate the compound word.  Forms such as this one are a feature restricted to LBH and are especially common in the books of Chronicles and Ezra.  (See *IBHS* section 19.7.c.)

נָטָה־לָו אֹהֶל בִּירוּשָׁלָֽם׃

5 וּמִזְבַּ֣ח הַנְּחֹ֗שֶׁת[8] אֲשֶׁ֤ר עָשָׂה֙ בְּצַלְאֵ֣ל בֶּן־אוּרִ֣י בֶן־ח֔וּר שָׂ֛ם[9] לִפְנֵ֖י מִשְׁכַּ֑ן

יְהוָ֑ה וַיִּדְרְשֵׁ֥הוּ[10] שְׁלֹמֹ֖ה וְהַקָּהָֽל׃

6 וַיַּ֣עַל שְׁלֹמֹ֣ה שָׁ֠ם עַל־מִזְבַּ֨ח הַנְּחֹ֜שֶׁת לִפְנֵ֣י יְהוָ֗ה אֲשֶׁ֛ר לָאֹ֥הֶל[11] מוֹעֵ֑ד

וַיַּ֧עַל[12] עָלָ֛יו עֹל֖וֹת אָֽלֶף׃

---

[8] What type of genitive construction is represented by this construct phrase? (See *IBHS* section 9.5.3.)

[9] Note that this is, as it stands in the Masoretic Text, a verb. How would you parse and translate it? Consult the text critical note. What other possible reading does it imply?

[10] Different translations (e.g., RSV vs. ESV) give different identifications of the antecedent of the object pronoun attached to this verb. What are the options from the narrative to which this object pronoun could refer? Which do you think is the best option and why?

[11] What use of לְ is this? (See section 11.5.)

[12] Is this verb in the Qal or Hiphil? How do you know?

7    בַּלַּ֣יְלָה הַה֔וּא נִרְאָ֥ה אֱלֹהִ֖ים לִשְׁלֹמֹ֑ה וַיֹּ֣אמֶר ל֔וֹ שְׁאַ֖ל מָ֥ה אֶתֶּן־לָֽךְ:[13]

8    וַיֹּ֤אמֶר שְׁלֹמֹה֙ לֵֽאלֹהִ֔ים[14] אַתָּ֗ה עָשִׂ֛יתָ עִם־דָּוִ֥יד[15] אָבִ֖י חֶ֥סֶד[16] גָּד֑וֹל

וְהִמְלַכְתַּ֖נִי[17] תַּחְתָּֽיו:

9    עַתָּה֙ יְהוָ֣ה אֱלֹהִ֔ים יֵֽאָמֵן֙ דְּבָ֣רְךָ֔ עִ֖ם דָּוִ֣יד אָבִ֑י כִּ֚י אַתָּ֣ה הִמְלַכְתַּ֔נִי עַל־עַ֕ם

רַ֖ב כַּעֲפַ֥ר הָאָֽרֶץ:

---

[13] The pronoun here is still 2ms.  How do you explain this form, which appears to match the 2fs form from your paradigms?  (See section 13.5.)

[14] The first vowel is a special case of the rule of *shewa*.  (See section 6.4.)

[15] Note the spelling of this name.  In Chronicles "David" is always written with full spelling, whereas in Samuel and Kings it is almost always written with defective spelling.  (See section 2.6.)

[16] Review your lexical research on this word from 2 Samuel 9:1.  How would you translate it, given that you cannot convey all of that meaning with a single English word?  How would you explain the term if you were teaching this passage?

[17] Note that this is an unconverted perfect (contra section 12.3), another LBH feature.  What verbal form would be used here if this were a CBH text?

10 עַתָּ֞ה חָכְמָ֤ה וּמַדָּע֙[18] תֶּן־לִ֔י וְאֵֽצְאָ֥ה[19] לִפְנֵ֥י הָֽעָם־הַזֶּ֖ה וְאָב֑וֹאָה כִּי־מִ֞י

יִשְׁפֹּ֛ט[20] אֶת־עַמְּךָ֥ הַזֶּ֖ה הַגָּד֑וֹל׃ ס[21]

11 וַיֹּ֤אמֶר אֱלֹהִים֙ לִשְׁלֹמֹ֔ה[22] יַ֣עַן אֲשֶׁר֩[23] הָיְתָ֨ה זֹ֜את עִם־לְבָבֶ֗ךָ וְלֹֽא־שָׁאַ֡לְתָּ

עֹ֩שֶׁר֩ נְכָסִ֨ים וְכָב֜וֹד וְאֵ֣ת ׀ נֶ֣פֶשׁ שֹׂנְאֶ֗יךָ[24] וְגַם־יָמִ֤ים רַבִּים֙ לֹ֣א שָׁאָ֔לְתָּ וַתִּֽשְׁאַל־לְךָ֛

---

[18] This is another LBH loanword.  Consult your lexicon.  From which language did it come into Biblical Hebrew?

[19] What is the relationship between this verb and the preceding verb?  (See section 25.7.)  III-ה verbs rarely show an explicit cohortative marker like the one you see on this form.

[20] Look at the parallel passage in 1 Kings 3:9. What verbal form has this imperfect replaced?

[21] This letter stands for *setuma*, the end of a segment in an ancient reading tradition of the Hebrew Bible.

[22] The vowel under the preposition לְ is the more classic application of the rule of *shewa*.  (See section 6.4.)

[23] Treat this word with the preceding יַעַן.  Check the lexicon under יַעַן if necessary.

[24] This form is a possessive suffix attached to a participle.  Parse and translate it.

חָכְמָ֤ה וּמַדָּע֙ אֲשֶׁ֣ר[25] תִּשְׁפּוֹט֙ אֶת־עַמִּ֔י אֲשֶׁ֥ר הִמְלַכְתִּ֖יךָ עָלָֽיו[26]׃

12　הַֽחָכְמָ֤ה וְהַמַּדָּע֙ נָת֣וּן לָ֔ךְ[27] וְעֹ֨שֶׁר וּנְכָסִ֤ים וְכָבוֹד֙ אֶתֶּן־לָ֔ךְ אֲשֶׁ֣ר לֹא־הָ֗יָה

כֵ֤ן לַמְּלָכִים֙ אֲשֶׁ֣ר לְפָנֶ֔יךָ וְאַחֲרֶ֖יךָ לֹ֥א יִֽהְיֶה־כֵּֽן׃

13　וַיָּבֹ֣א שְׁלֹמֹ֡ה לַבָּמָ֣ה[28] אֲשֶׁר־בְּגִבְעוֹן֩ יְרוּשָׁלִַ֨ם מִלִּפְנֵ֜י אֹ֤הֶל מוֹעֵד֙ וַיִּמְלֹ֖ךְ

עַל־יִשְׂרָאֵֽל׃ פ[29]

---

[25] In CBH this would likely be לְמַ֫עַן. What translation should you give to אֲשֶׁר here?

[26] Note that this is a resumptive pronoun. (See section 11.4.)

[27] See verse 7.

[28] Consult the text critical note. How do the various versions read for this word?

[29] See 2 Samuel 9:13.

14 וַיֶּאֱסֹף שְׁלֹמֹה רֶכֶב וּפָרָשִׁים[30] וַיְהִי־לֹו אֶלֶף וְאַרְבַּע־מֵאֹות רֶכֶב וּשְׁנֵים־

עָשָׂר אֶלֶף פָּרָשִׁים וַיַּנִּיחֵם בְּעָרֵי הָרֶכֶב וְעִם־הַמֶּלֶךְ בִּירוּשָׁלָ͏ִם׃

15 וַיִּתֵּן[31] הַמֶּלֶךְ אֶת־הַכֶּסֶף[32] וְאֶת־הַזָּהָב בִּירוּשָׁלַ͏ִם כָּאֲבָנִים[33] וְאֵת הָאֲרָזִים

נָתַן כַּשִּׁקְמִים אֲשֶׁר־בַּשְּׁפֵלָה לָרֹב׃

---

[30] This homonym can indicate either horses or horsemen.

[31] The most common gloss of נתן is "to give," but that gloss does not seem to work as well here. What gloss would you prefer and why?

[32] This is a generic use of the definite article, used to mark a type of thing. English typically represents this with the anarthrous form–not "the silver," but "silver." (See *IBHS* 13.5.1.f.)

[33] What use of כ is this? (See *IBHS* section 11.2.9.)

16 וּמוֹצָ֧א הַסּוּסִ֛ים אֲשֶׁ֥ר לִשְׁלֹמֹ֖ה מִמִּצְרָ֑יִם וּמִקְוֵ֤א[34] סֹחֲרֵ֣י הַמֶּ֔לֶךְ מִקְוֵ֖א

יִקְח֥וּ בִמְחִֽיר[35]׃

17 וַֽ֠יַּעֲלוּ[36] וַיּוֹצִ֨יאוּ מִמִּצְרַ֤יִם מֶרְכָּבָה֙ בְּשֵׁשׁ֙[37] מֵא֣וֹת כֶּ֔סֶף וְס֖וּס בַּחֲמִשִּׁ֣ים

וּמֵאָ֑ה וְ֠כֵן לְכָל־מַלְכֵ֧י הַֽחִתִּ֛ים וּמַלְכֵ֥י אֲרָ֖ם בְּיָדָ֥ם יוֹצִֽיאוּ[38]׃

---

[34] This is וּ plus מִן plus a proper noun. Note that the text critical note suggests moving the *athnach* to this word. How would doing so impact your translation of the verse?

[35] What use of בְּ is this? (See *IBHS* section 11.2.5.)

[36] This could formally be a Qal or a Hiphil. Which makes more sense in context?

[37] What use of the preposition בְּ is this? (See *IBHS* section 11.2.5.)

[38] Consult a Bible atlas to identify the location of these nations. How does this help you understand the riches generated under Solomon's reign?

18 וַיֹּאמֶר[39] שְׁלֹמֹה לִבְנוֹת בַּיִת֙ לְשֵׁם֙ יְהוָ֔ה וּבַ֖יִת לְמַלְכוּתֽוֹ׃

---

[39] It is an LBH usage of אמר to indicate giving orders.

# ה (5) 

Nehemiah 1 gives a second example of Late Biblical Hebrew, giving you further practice with the different language expectations you should bring to a LBH text.

1    דִּבְרֵי נְחֶמְיָה בֶּן־חֲכַלְיָה וַיְהִי בְחֹדֶשׁ־ כִּסְלֵו[1] שְׁנַת עֶשְׂרִים וַאֲנִי הָיִיתִי[2]

בְּשׁוּשַׁן הַבִּירָה:

2    וַיָּבֹא חֲנָנִי אֶחָד מֵאַחַי הוּא וַאֲנָשִׁים מִיהוּדָה[3] וָאֶשְׁאָלֵם עַל־הַיְּהוּדִים

---

[1] Note the Qere reading.  The Qetiv spelling is what would be expected in the Persian period.  The Qere's י may be present to protect the consonantal value of the ו against possible misvocalizations.

[2] CBH would use a verbless circumstantial clause to convey this idea. (See section 15.8.)  LBH tends to use the verb היה much more often, including in places where CBH would use a verbless clause.

[3] Most English translations end the first sentence of the passage here, breaking the thought at a different place than the Masoretic vocalization.  (See section 11.8.)

הַפְּלֵיטָה⁴ אֲשֶׁר־נִשְׁאֲרוּ מִן־הַשֶּׁבִי וְעַל־יְרוּשָׁלָ͏ִם׃

3  וַיֹּאמְרוּ לִי הַנִּשְׁאָרִ֔ים אֲשֶׁר־נִשְׁאֲרוּ מִן־הַשְּׁבִי שָׁם בַּמְּדִינָה בְּרָעָה גְדֹלָה

וּבְחֶרְפָּה וְחוֹמַת יְרוּשָׁלַ͏ִם מְפֹרָצֶת⁵ וּשְׁעָרֶיהָ נִצְּתוּ בָאֵשׁ׃

4  וַיְהִי כְּשָׁמְעִי⁶ אֶת־הַדְּבָרִים הָאֵלֶּה יָשַׁבְתִּי⁷ וָאֶבְכֶּה וָאֶתְאַבְּלָה⁸ יָמִים

---

⁴ Note the feminine singular noun following a masculine plural noun.  This indicates an instance of apposition between two nouns.  If פְּלֵיטָה were an adjective, it would have to agree in gender and number.

⁵ What is the relationship between the Pual of this verb and the Qal? (See sections 14.1, 15.1, and 20.10.)
Why is this participle vocalized with a qameṣ instead of a segol?  (See section 13.5.)

⁶ Be careful to pronounce the first full vowel correctly, which will aid you in parsing this form.  (See sections 2.5 and 13.3.)

⁷ LBH uses a perfect verbal form here, where CBH would use a narrative form.

⁸ This form is not cohortative, as the prefixes indicate it is a narrative.  First person narrative forms will often have a ה ending, quite possibly by analogy with cohortatives.

וָאֱהִ֥י צָם֖[9] וּמִתְפַּלֵּ֑ל לִפְנֵ֖י אֱלֹהֵ֥י הַשָּׁמָֽיִם׃

5     וָאֹמַ֗ר[10] אָֽנָּ֤א יְהוָה֙ אֱלֹהֵ֣י הַשָּׁמַ֔יִם הָאֵ֥ל הַגָּד֖וֹל וְהַנּוֹרָ֑א שֹׁמֵ֤ר הַבְּרִית֙

וָחֶ֔סֶד לְאֹהֲבָ֖יו וּלְשֹׁמְרֵ֥י מִצְוֺתָֽיו׃

6     תְּהִ֣י נָ֣א אָזְנְךָֽ־קַשֶּׁ֣בֶת[11] וְֽעֵינֶ֣יךָ פְתֻוּחֹות[12] לִשְׁמֹ֙עַ֙ אֶל־תְּפִלַּ֣ת עַבְדְּךָ֗ אֲשֶׁ֨ר

---

[9] The combination of היה plus a participle (what is called a *periphrastic form*) is quite common in LBH.

[10] The following prayer uses very traditional language, much of which linguistically matches the Deuteronomistic literature.

[11] Check in your lexicon for the occurrences of this adjective and the related vocalization of קֶשֶׁב. Are these LBH works, CBH works, or both?

[12] The BHS text reproduces the Leningrad Codex, even if that manuscript has an error or irregularity. Note that the u-class vowel here is doubly marked, with both a *qibbuṣ* and a *shureq*. Note the BHS text critical apparatus, which indicates that many manuscripts have no *qibbuṣ*.

31

אָנֹכִי[13] מִתְפַּלֵּל לְפָנֶיךָ הַיּוֹם יוֹמָם וָלַיְלָה עַל־בְּנֵי יִשְׂרָאֵל עֲבָדֶיךָ

וּמִתְוַדֶּה[14] עַל־חַטֹּאות בְּנֵי־יִשְׂרָאֵל אֲשֶׁר חָטָאנוּ לָךְ וַאֲנִי וּבֵית־אָבִי

חָטָאנוּ:

7    חָבֹל[15] חָבַלְנוּ לָךְ וְלֹא־שָׁמַרְנוּ אֶת־הַמִּצְוֺת וְאֶת־הַחֻקִּים וְאֶת־הַמִּשְׁפָּטִים

---

[13] The use of the long form of the 1cs pronoun here (as opposed to אֲנִי) is very rare in LBH. It is probably used here as an anachronistic phrasing due to the liturgical context of prayer.

[14] The verbal root for this form is difficult to identify. Remember that I-י verbs were originally I-ו and that the ו reappears when "trapped" by a prefix. (See section 27.2.) What could explain the missing third root letter? What is the root and what is the parsing of this verb?

[15] How should this form be parsed as it is currently vocalized? If this were a CBH passage, how would you suggest revocalizing it? (See section 16.10.) In LBH, the infinitive construct often takes on the role of the infinitive absolute, so a revocalization is not necessary here.

אֲשֶׁ֣ר צִוִּ֔יתָ אֶת־מֹשֶׁ֖ה עַבְדֶּֽךָ׃

8    זְכָר־נָא֙ אֶת־הַדָּבָ֔ר אֲשֶׁ֥ר צִוִּ֖יתָ אֶת־מֹשֶׁ֣ה עַבְדְּךָ֣ לֵאמֹ֑ר[16] אַתֶּ֣ם[17] תִּמְעָ֔לוּ

אֲנִ֕י[18] אָפִ֥יץ אֶתְכֶ֖ם בָּעַמִּֽים׃

9    וְשַׁבְתֶּ֣ם[19] אֵלַ֔י וּשְׁמַרְתֶּם֙ מִצְוֺתַ֔י וַעֲשִׂיתֶ֖ם אֹתָ֑ם אִם־יִהְיֶ֣ה[20] נִֽדַּחֲכֶ֗ם[21]

---

[16] What follows is not an exact quotation but instead reminiscent language.

[17] Note from the BHS text critical note that some versions suggest that the word אִם may have dropped out due to haplography.

[18] LBH commonly has an asyndetic apodosis (not marked with וְ) for if . . . then statements.

[19] Do not let the verse numbers blind you to the flow of the passage.  Continue the thought of this verse from verse 8.

[20] Note again the LBH tendency to use היה more frequently than CBH.

[21] This is a participle form with a possessive suffix.  How is it parsed?

בִּקְצֵה הַשָּׁמַ֫יִם מִשָּׁם[22] אֲקַבְּצֵ֗ם וַהֲבִיאֹתִים[23] אֶל־הַמָּק֗וֹם אֲשֶׁר בָּחַ֫רְתִּי

לְשַׁכֵּן אֶת־שְׁמִי שָׁם:

10     וְהֵם[24] עֲבָדֶ֫יךָ וְעַמֶּ֑ךָ אֲשֶׁר פָּדִ֫יתָ בְּכֹחֲךָ הַגָּד֑וֹל וּבְיָדְךָ הַחֲזָקָה:

11     אָנָּא אֲדֹנָי תְּהִי נָא אָזְנְךָ־קַשֶּׁ֫בֶת אֶל־תְּפִלַּת עַבְדְּךָ וְאֶל־תְּפִלַּת עֲבָדֶ֫יךָ

הַחֲפֵצִים֙ לְיִרְאָה אֶת־שְׁמֶ֔ךָ וְהַצְלִ֫יחָה[25]־נָּא לְעַבְדְּךָ הַיּ֗וֹם וּתְנֵ֫הוּ

---

[22] Note again the LBH tendency toward the lack of a וֹ in the apodosis of the if . . . then statement.

[23] Note the qetiv/qere on this word.

[24] Note the word order.  What type of clause is this? (See section 15.8.)  This clause provides the basis for Nehemiah's request.

[25] For the ה, see section 21.7, note 26.  (See also section 7.3.)

לְרַחֲמִ֖ים [26] לִפְנֵ֖י הָאִ֣ישׁ הַזֶּ֑ה וַאֲנִ֥י [27] הָיִ֖יתִי מַשְׁקֶ֥ה לַמֶּֽלֶךְ׃ פ

---

[27] Note that Nehemiah 1 closes with a certain type of clause.  What is the word order, and what is this type of clause?  (See section 15.8.)  Why has this information been held back until the end of the narrative?

# PART II

---

# Readings in Legal Texts

Leviticus 1 gives a first example of legal literature, this example being from the priestly literature, the handbook for sacrificial offerings.  The syntax of Leviticus will be relatively easy, as there is a more continuous theme running through the text.  The vocabulary, however, will be less familiar as you deal with the specific details of the burnt offering and the various pieces of the animals involved.

1    וַיִּקְרָ֖א אֶל־מֹשֶׁ֑ה וַיְדַבֵּ֤ר יְהוָה֙ אֵלָ֔יו מֵאֹ֥הֶל מוֹעֵ֖ד לֵאמֹֽר׃

2    דַּבֵּ֞ר אֶל־בְּנֵ֤י יִשְׂרָאֵל֙ וְאָמַרְתָּ֣ אֲלֵהֶ֔ם אָדָ֗ם כִּֽי־יַקְרִ֥יב מִכֶּ֛ם קָרְבָּ֖ן[1]

לַֽיהוָ֑ה[2] מִן־הַבְּהֵמָ֗ה[3] מִן־הַבָּקָר֙ וּמִן־הַצֹּ֔אן תַּקְרִ֖יבוּ אֶת־קָרְבַּנְכֶֽם׃

---

[1] What is the semantic range of this term in its use here?  (See section 5.7.)  Note that this range is broader than the specific use of the designation referenced in Mark 7:11.

[2] Break the clause here, with the *athnach*, grouping the remainder of the verse into a second clause.  What modality do you assign to the second clause in this verse?  Why?  (See section 5.2.)  This modality for the imperfect is common in legal literature.

[3] This noun is often glossed as "cattle," but the context of this passage makes it clear that it actually has a broader semantic range.  How would you define the semantic range of the term?

3 אִם־עֹלָה קָרְבָּנוֹ מִן־הַבָּקָר זָכָר תָּמִים יַקְרִיבֶנּוּ⁴ אֶל־פֶּתַח אֹהֶל מוֹעֵד

יַקְרִיב אֹתוֹ לִרְצֹנוֹ⁵ לִפְנֵי יְהוָה:

4 וְסָמַךְ⁶ יָדוֹ עַל רֹאשׁ הָעֹלָה וְנִרְצָה לוֹ⁷ לְכַפֵּר עָלָיו:

5 וְשָׁחַט⁸ אֶת־בֶּן הַבָּקָר לִפְנֵי יְהוָה וְהִקְרִיבוּ בְּנֵי אַהֲרֹן הַכֹּהֲנִים אֶת־הַדָּם

---

⁴ Is the modality of this verb the same or different from the modality of תַּקְרִיבוּ in verse 2? Why do you make that choice?

⁵ What is the sense of this possessive suffix on the noun? How do you know?

⁶ To which verb do you look to get the sense of this converted perfect?

⁷ Is the antecedent to this pronoun the one who brings the burnt offering or the burnt offering itself? How do you know? Use a lexicon to check the use of this verbal root with ל to help you distinguish the correct meaning.

⁸ Consult a research lexicon and other lexical resources to determine the semantic range of this term. How does it correspond to the terms זבח and הרג? (See section 5.7.)

וְזָרְק֨וּ אֶת־הַדָּ֤ם עַל־הַמִּזְבֵּ֙חַ֙ סָבִ֔יב אֲשֶׁר־פֶּ֖תַח אֹ֥הֶל מוֹעֵֽד׃

6   וְהִפְשִׁ֖יט אֶת־הָעֹלָ֑ה וְנִתַּ֥ח אֹתָ֖הּ לִנְתָחֶֽיהָ׃[9]

7   וְנָתְנ֜וּ[10] בְּנֵ֨י אַהֲרֹ֧ן הַכֹּהֵ֛ן אֵ֖שׁ עַל־הַמִּזְבֵּ֑חַ וְעָרְכ֥וּ עֵצִ֖ים עַל־הָאֵֽשׁ׃

8   וְעָרְכ֗וּ בְּנֵ֤י אַהֲרֹן֙ הַכֹּ֣הֲנִ֔ים אֵ֚ת הַנְּתָחִ֔ים אֶת־הָרֹ֖אשׁ וְאֶת־הַפָּ֑דֶר עַל־

הָֽעֵצִים֙ אֲשֶׁ֣ר עַל־הָאֵ֔שׁ אֲשֶׁ֖ר עַל־הַמִּזְבֵּֽחַ׃

---

[9] Why is this possessive suffix feminine, even though בָּקָר is a masculine noun?

[10] "Give" would here be a poor English gloss for the use of נתן in context. Based on your lexicon, what gloss would be better? Why do you pick that portion of the semantic range of נתן? (See section 6.7.)

9 וְקִרְבּוֹ וּכְרָעָיו¹¹ יִרְחַץ בַּמָּיִם וְהִקְטִיר הַכֹּהֵן אֶת־הַכֹּל הַמִּזְבֵּחָה¹² עֹלָה

אִשֵּׁה¹³ רֵיחַ־נִיחוֹחַ¹⁴ לַיהוָה: ס¹⁵

10 וְאִם־מִן־הַצֹּאן קָרְבָּנוֹ מִן־הַכְּשָׂבִים אוֹ מִן־הָעִזִּים לְעֹלָה זָכָר תָּמִים

יַקְרִיבֶנּוּ:

---

¹¹ This relatively rare noun has been variously glossed as "feet," "shins," or "hind legs." Which gloss do you prefer and why?

¹² Make sure you correctly note the ה on the end of the word to obtain the correct translation. (See section 8.9.)

¹³ This term traditionally is translated "fire offering," however commentators have noted that the entirety of the אִשֶּׁה is not burned up in later chapters (e.g., 2:3, 7:30, etc.).

¹⁴ What is the genitive relationship expressed by this construct phrase? (See *IBHS* section 9.5.)

¹⁵ See 2 Chronicles 1:10.

11 וְשָׁחַ֨ט אֹת֜וֹ עַ֣ל יֶ֧רֶךְ[16] הַמִּזְבֵּ֛חַ צָפֹ֖נָה לִפְנֵ֣י יְהוָ֑ה וְזָרְק֡וּ בְּנֵי֩ אַהֲרֹ֨ן הַכֹּהֲנִ֜ים

אֶת־דָּמ֛וֹ עַל־הַמִּזְבֵּ֖חַ סָבִֽיב׃

12 וְנִתַּ֤ח אֹתוֹ֙ לִנְתָחָ֔יו וְאֶת־רֹאשׁ֖וֹ וְאֶת־פִּדְר֑וֹ וְעָרַ֤ךְ הַכֹּהֵן֙ אֹתָ֔ם עַל־הָ֣עֵצִ֔ים

אֲשֶׁר֙ עַל־הָאֵ֔שׁ אֲשֶׁ֖ר עַל־הַמִּזְבֵּֽחַ׃

13 וְהַקֶּ֥רֶב וְהַכְּרָעַ֖יִם יִרְחַ֣ץ בַּמָּ֑יִם וְהִקְרִ֨יב הַכֹּהֵ֤ן אֶת־הַכֹּל֙ וְהִקְטִ֣יר

---

[16] What is the semantic range of this word?  Which portion is contextually appropriate here?  (See sections 5.7 and 6.7.)

הַמִּזְבֵּ֔חָה עֹלָ֣ה ה֗וּא אִשֵּׁ֛ה רֵ֥יחַ נִיחֹ֖חַ לַיהוָֽה׃ פ

14 וְאִ֧ם מִן־הָע֛וֹף עֹלָ֥ה קָרְבָּנ֖וֹ לַֽיהוָ֑ה וְהִקְרִ֣יב מִן־הַתֹּרִ֗ים א֛וֹ מִן־בְּנֵ֥י הַיּוֹנָ֖ה

אֶת־קָרְבָּנֽוֹ׃

15 וְהִקְרִיב֤וֹ הַכֹּהֵן֙ אֶל־הַמִּזְבֵּ֔חַ וּמָלַק֙ אֶת־רֹאשׁ֔וֹ וְהִקְטִ֖יר הַמִּזְבֵּ֑חָה וְנִמְצָ֣ה

דָמ֔וֹ עַ֖ל קִ֥יר הַמִּזְבֵּֽחַ׃

16 וְהֵסִ֥יר אֶת־מֻרְאָת֖וֹ בְּנֹצָתָ֑הּ[17] וְהִשְׁלִיךְ֩ אֹתָ֨הּ אֵ֤צֶל הַמִּזְבֵּ֙חַ֙ קֵ֔דְמָה אֶל־

מְק֖וֹם הַדָּֽשֶׁן׃[18]

17 וְשִׁסַּ֨ע אֹת֣וֹ בִכְנָפָיו֮ לֹ֣א יַבְדִּיל֒ וְהִקְטִ֨יר אֹת֤וֹ הַכֹּהֵן֙ הַמִּזְבֵּ֔חָה עַל־הָעֵצִ֖ים

אֲשֶׁ֣ר עַל־הָאֵ֑שׁ עֹלָ֣ה ה֗וּא אִשֵּׁ֛ה רֵ֥יחַ נִיחֹ֖חַ לַיהוָֽה׃ ס

---

[17] This form occurs only here in the Old Testament/Hebrew Bible, making it a *hapax legomenon*. What are your sources for determining its meaning and appropriate gloss? What choice would you make and why? (See sections 22.9 and 23.6.)

[18] דשׁן typically glosses as "fat" or "juicy." How is it that most English translations say "the place for the ashes" for אֶל־מְק֖וֹם הַדָּֽשֶׁן?

Deuteronomy 22 is a the first of two examples of reading in the Deuteronomistic legal literature.  At times (as in verses 1-4) several verses will go together to cover a single legal area.  At other times, each verse will cover a different law with seemingly little order or connection between it and the laws that precede and follow.  Because of this lack of connection, context is less helpful in determining the correct gloss for various words, and the skills of lexical analysis are particularly important.  (See sections 5.7 and 6.7.)  You will also want to pay attention to the various uses of כִּי that you encounter in the text.  (See section 14.10.)

1  לֹא¹־תִרְאֶה֩ אֶת־שׁ֨וֹר אָחִ֜יךָ א֤וֹ אֶת־שֵׂיוֹ֙ נִדָּחִ֔ים² וְהִתְעַלַּמְתָּ֖ מֵהֶ֑ם³ הָשֵׁ֣ב

תְּשִׁיבֵ֖ם⁴ לְאָחִֽיךָ׃

---

¹ The scope of negation covers the whole of the first half of the verse, up to the *athnach*.
² This modifies the previous word, which is clearly definite (both because it has a possessive pronoun and because it is marked by the definite direct object marker–see section 4.6).  This participle, then, cannot be functioning attributively.  Why not?  (See sections 4.6 and 9.5.)  How, then, is this participle functioning in relation to the previous word?
³ The use of מֵן with the verb indicates a specific gloss is appropriate.  Check your lexicon to determine the correct gloss.  Survey the other uses of this root.  What type of "hiding" do they all reference?
⁴ The first vowel in this verb has reduced due to the addition of the object suffix.  What would the vowel have been before it reduced?  (See sections 21.2, 21.4, and 26.6).

2    וְאִם־לֹא קָרוֹב אָחִ֫יךָ⁵ אֵלֶ֫יךָ וְלֹא יְדַעְתּוֹ⁶ וַאֲסַפְתּוֹ⁷ אֶל־תּוֹךְ בֵּיתֶ֫ךָ וְהָיָה

עִמְּךָ עַד דְּרֹשׁ אָחִ֫יךָ⁸ אֹתוֹ וַהֲשֵׁבֹתוֹ⁹ לוֹ׃

3    וְכֵן תַּעֲשֶׂה לַחֲמֹרוֹ וְכֵן תַּעֲשֶׂה לְשִׂמְלָתוֹ וְכֵן תַּעֲשֶׂה לְכָל־אֲבֵדַת¹⁰

---

⁵ Given this second verse, what portion of the semantic range of אִם is intended in Deuteronomy 22? How do you know? (See sections 5.7 and 6.7.)

⁶ The addition of the object suffix has caused the loss of the vowel that typically ends this verbal form. What would the form be without the suffix? (See section 21.2.)

⁷ The syntax of the converted perfect explained in section 12.3 largely covered the usage of the converted perfect in narrative texts. The sequence expressed by the converted perfect can be quite flexible. For example, here the וֹ indicates the apodosis of the "if/then" construction that begins with אִם. The sequence is "If . . . , then you may . . ." (See *IBHS* 32.2.3.)

⁸ Is this the subject or the object of the preceding infinitive construct? Given the next word in the clause, how do you know?

⁹ The modality of this verb changes. The previous two converted perfects indicated a sequence after אִם that involved permission ("you may..."). What is the modality of this third converted perfect?

¹⁰ This is not the noun עֶ֫בֶד. Use your lexicon to determine the correct gloss.

אָחִ֙יךָ֙[11] אֲשֶׁר־תֹּאבַד֙[12] מִמֶּ֔נּוּ וּמְצָאתָ֖הּ[13] לֹ֥א תוּכַ֖ל לְהִתְעַלֵּֽם׃ ס

4    לֹֽא־תִרְאֶה֩ אֶת־חֲמ֨וֹר אָחִ֜יךָ א֤וֹ[14] שׁוֹרוֹ֙ נֹפְלִ֣ים בַּדֶּ֔רֶךְ וְהִתְעַלַּמְתָּ֖ מֵהֶ֑ם

הָקֵ֥ם תָּקִ֖ים עִמּֽוֹ׃ ס

5    לֹא־יִהְיֶ֤ה כְלִי־גֶ֙בֶר֙ עַל־אִשָּׁ֔ה וְלֹא־יִלְבַּ֥שׁ גֶּ֖בֶר שִׂמְלַ֣ת אִשָּׁ֑ה כִּ֥י[15] תוֹעֲבַ֛ת

---

[11] This construct phrase expresses the genitive relation. Which use of the genitive does it convey? (See *IBHS* section 9.5.1.)

[12] Formally, this verb could be either 3fs or 2ms. Which one is a preferable reading and why?

[13] Remember the function of the *mappiq*. (See section 2.6.)

[14] Check the text critical note in BHS. If the word אֵת were original to the text and has dropped out of the Masoretic Text, what text critical process could explain that occurrence? If you consider the Masoretic Text more likely the original reading, how would you explain the addition of אֵת in the other witnesses?

[15] What use of כִּי is this? (See section 14.10.)

יְהוָ֥ה אֱלֹהֶ֖יךָ כָּל־עֹשֵׂ֥ה אֵֽלֶּה: פ

6   כִּ֣י[16] יִקָּרֵ֣א קַן־צִפּ֣וֹר ׀ לְפָנֶ֡יךָ בַּדֶּ֜רֶךְ בְּכָל־עֵ֣ץ ׀ א֣וֹ עַל־הָאָ֗רֶץ אֶפְרֹחִים֙ א֣וֹ

בֵיצִ֔ים וְהָאֵ֤ם רֹבֶ֙צֶת֙ עַל־הָֽאֶפְרֹחִ֔ים א֖וֹ עַל־הַבֵּיצִ֑ים לֹא־תִקַּ֥ח הָאֵ֖ם עַל־[17]

הַבָּנִֽים:[18]

---

[16] This is a different use of כִּי. (See section 14.10.)

[17] Which use of עַל is this? (See *IBHS* section 11.2.13.)

[18] Which portion of the semantic range of בֵּן is intended here?

7     שַׁלֵּחַ תְּשַׁלַּח¹⁹ אֶת־הָאֵ֗ם וְאֶת־הַבָּנִ֖ים תִּֽקַּֽח־²⁰לָ֑ךְ²¹ לְמַ֙עַן֙ יִ֣יטַב לָ֔ךְ²²

וְהַאֲרַכְתָּ֖ יָמִֽים׃ ס

8     כִּ֤י²³ תִבְנֶה֙ בַּ֣יִת חָדָ֔שׁ וְעָשִׂ֥יתָ²⁴ מַעֲקֶ֖ה לְגַגֶּ֑ךָ וְלֹֽא־תָשִׂ֤ים²⁵ דָּמִים֙²⁶ בְּבֵיתֶ֔ךָ

כִּֽי²⁷־יִפֹּ֥ל הַנֹּפֵ֖ל מִמֶּֽנּוּ׃ ס

---

¹⁹ What is signified by the choice of the Piel form of שׁלח? (See section 20.10.)

²⁰ What modality is indicated by this imperfect form? (See section 5.2.)

²¹ What gender is the pronoun attached to the preposition? (See section 13.5.)

²² Pausal forms are less likely with lesser disjunctive accents, but–as here–they clearly can occur.

²³ See the note on verse 6.

²⁴ The converted perfect again indicates a sequence. Given the initial כִּ of the verse, what type of sequence is intended? (See *IBHS* section 32.2.3.)

²⁵ What type of sequence is indicated by the ו that leads off this verbal phrase?

²⁶ What portion of the semantic range of דָּם is indicated here?

²⁷ What use of כִּי is this? (See section 14.10.)

9    לֹא־תִזְרַ֥ע²⁸ כַּרְמְךָ֖ כִּלְאָ֑יִם פֶּן־תִּקְדַּ֗שׁ הַֽמְלֵאָ֤ה הַזֶּ֙רַע֙ אֲשֶׁ֣ר תִּזְרָ֔ע וּתְבוּאַ֖ת

הַכָּֽרֶם׃²⁹ ס

10    לֹֽא־תַחֲרֹ֥שׁ בְּשׁוֹר־וּבַחֲמֹ֖ר יַחְדָּֽו׃ ס

11    לֹ֤א תִלְבַּשׁ֙ שַֽׁעַטְנֵ֔ז³⁰ צֶ֥מֶר וּפִשְׁתִּ֖ים יַחְדָּֽו׃ ס

12    גְּדִלִ֖ים תַּעֲשֶׂה־לָּ֑ךְ עַל־אַרְבַּ֛ע כַּנְפ֥וֹת³¹ כְּסוּתְךָ֖ אֲשֶׁ֥ר תְּכַסֶּה־³²בָּֽהּ׃ ס

---

²⁸ What type of negation is indicated here?  (See section 7.8.)
²⁹ What type of genitive relationship does this construct phrase signify?  (See *IBHS* section 9.5.a.)
³⁰ This is not technically a *hapax legomenon*, as the word also occurs in Leviticus 19:19.  Consult a lexicon to determine the origin of this word.
³¹ What portion of the semantic range of כָּנָף is intended here?  How do you know?
³² Does the choice of the Piel for this root have exegetical significance?  (See section 20.10.)

Deuteronomy 24 gives a second example of the Deuteronomistic legal literature, showing many of the same features as seen in the previous selection. Continue to pay particular attention to the usage of כִּי. Further, note the variety of sequences that can be conveyed by the converted perfect.

1    כִּי[1]־יִקַּח אִישׁ אִשָּׁה וּבְעָלָהּ[2] וְהָיָה אִם־לֹא תִמְצָא־חֵן בְּעֵינָיו כִּי־מָצָא בָהּ

עֶרְוַת דָּבָר[3] וְכָתַב לָהּ סֵפֶר כְּרִיתֻת וְנָתַן בְּיָדָהּ[4] וְשִׁלְּחָהּ מִבֵּיתוֹ׃

2    וְיָצְאָה מִבֵּיתוֹ וְהָלְכָה וְהָיְתָה לְאִישׁ־אַחֵר׃

---

[1] For this and all following uses of כִּי, consult section 14.10 carefully.

[2] You should be used to the function of the *mappiq* at this point. If necessary, review chapters 2 and 5.

[3] This construct phrase is often translated "some indecency." Consult the other references in your lexicon to determine the semantic range of this term–indecency of what type?

[4] In a legal context, the possession of the document gives the holder a right, in this case the right to remarry.

3    וּשְׂנֵאָהּ֮ הָאִ֣ישׁ הָאַחֲרוֹן֒ וְכָ֨תַב לָ֜הּ סֵ֤פֶר כְּרִיתֻת֙ וְנָתַ֣ן בְּיָדָ֔הּ וְשִׁלְּחָ֖הּ מִבֵּית֑וֹ

אֽוֹ כִ֤י יָמוּת֙ הָאִ֣ישׁ הָאַחֲר֔וֹן אֲשֶׁר־לְקָחָ֥הּ ל֖וֹ לְאִשָּֽׁה׃

4    לֹא־יוּכַ֣ל בַּעְלָ֣הּ הָרִאשׁ֣וֹן אֲשֶֽׁר־שִׁלְּחָ֣הּ לָשׁ֗וּב לְקַחְתָּהּ֙ לִהְי֣וֹת ל֣וֹ לְאִשָּׁ֔ה

אֲשֶׁר֙ יְהוָ֣ה אֱלֹהֶ֔יךָ נֹתֵ֥ן לְךָ֖ נַחֲלָֽה׃ ס

---

[5] Note that the converted perfects are still picking up their basic modality from the first verb in verse 1.

[6] This is the beginning of the apodosis. What sense of the verb יכל is appropriate here?

[7] The syntactical construction here is a form of שׁוב followed by another verb. Check your lexicon to determine what that construction indicates.

5  כִּי־יִקַּח אִישׁ אִשָּׁה חֲדָשָׁה לֹא יֵצֵא בַּצָּבָא וְלֹא־יַעֲבֹר עָלָיו⁸ לְכָל־דָּבָר⁹

נָקִי יִהְיֶה לְבֵיתוֹ שָׁנָה אֶחָת וְשִׂמַּח¹⁰ אֶת¹¹־אִשְׁתּוֹ אֲשֶׁר־לָקָח: ס

6  לֹא־יַחֲבֹל רֵחַיִם¹² וָרָכֶב¹³ כִּי־נֶפֶשׁ הוּא חֹבֵל:¹⁴ ס

7  כִּי־יִמָּצֵא אִישׁ גֹּנֵב נֶפֶשׁ¹⁵ מֵאֶחָיו מִבְּנֵי יִשְׂרָאֵל וְהִתְעַמֶּר־בּוֹ¹⁶ וּמְכָרוֹ וָמֵת

---

⁸ This is an idiomatic use of עבר על. Idioms are words or phrases that are used in a common way that does not match their literal meaning (e.g., "It's raining cats and dogs."). The idiomatic use of עבר על here is to have an obligation.

⁹ The text critical note in BHS suggests reading this phrase without the ל. If so, it would become the subject of the preceding verbal phrase.

¹⁰ The text critical note in BHS suggests reading with the Targumim and repointing this as what *binyan*? If so, how would your translation of the verbal phrase change? Which do you think is more likely correct?

¹¹ How does your decision on the parsing of the preceding verb change your gloss for this word?

¹² Why is this form dual? (See section 4.1.)

¹³ Carefully check the lexical entry for this word. It should not be glossed "chariot" here.

¹⁴ Which use of the participle is this? (See section 9.5.) Note that the BHS text critical note suggests an alternate reading. How would this verb be parsed if you accepted the alternate reading?

¹⁵ You should gloss this noun with the preceding verb and be slightly dynamic in your translation of these two words together. (See section 21.7.)

¹⁶ What use of בּ is this? (See *IBHS* section 11.2.5.f.)

הַגַּנָּב הַהוּא וּבִעַרְתָּ הָרָע מִקִּרְבֶּךָ׃

8 הִשָּׁמֶר בְּנֶגַע־הַצָּרַעַת לִשְׁמֹר מְאֹד וְלַעֲשׂוֹת כְּכֹל אֲשֶׁר־יוֹרוּ[17] אֶתְכֶם

הַכֹּהֲנִים הַלְוִיִּם כַּאֲשֶׁר צִוִּיתִם[18] תִּשְׁמְרוּ[19] לַעֲשׂוֹת׃ ס

9 זָכוֹר[20] אֵת אֲשֶׁר־עָשָׂה יְהוָה אֱלֹהֶיךָ לְמִרְיָם[21] בַּדֶּרֶךְ בְּצֵאתְכֶם

מִמִּצְרָיִם׃ ס

---

[17] Note that this is a doubly weak verb. (See sections 24.2 and 24.3.)

[18] Parse this word carefully, paying particular attention to the vowel under the ת.

[19] What modality would you assign to this imperfect? Why? (See section 5.2.)

[20] What use of the infinitive absolute is this? (See section 13.1.)

[21] This is a proper noun.

10 כִּי־תַשֶּׁה²² בְרֵעֲךָ מַשַּׁאת מְא֑וּמָה לֹא־תָבֹא אֶל־בֵּיתוֹ לַעֲבֹט עֲבֹטוֹ׃

11 בַּח֣וּץ תַּעֲמֹד וְהָא֗ישׁ אֲשֶׁ֤ר אַתָּה֙ נֹשֶׁ֣ה ב֔וֹ²³ יוֹצִ֥יא אֵלֶ֛יךָ אֶת־הַעֲב֖וֹט

הַחֽוּצָה׃

12 וְאִם־א֥ישׁ עָנִ֖י ה֑וּא²⁴ לֹ֣א תִשְׁכַּ֖ב בַּעֲבֹטֽוֹ׃²⁵

---

²² This is another doubly weak verb. Note that it is a form of the root נשא, not נשה. Forms with the ה ending occur due to the similarly weak sounds of /h/ and the unvoiced glottal stop of א.

²³ What use of בּ is this? (See *IBHS* section 11.2.5.)

²⁴ Is this verbless clause identifying or descriptive? How do you know? (See section 15.8.)

²⁵ This phrasing will make sense once you translate verse 13 and identify what the pledge for the loan is.

13 הָשֵׁב֩ תָּשִׁ֨יב ל֤וֹ אֶֽת־הַעֲבוֹט֙ כְּבֹא֮²⁶ הַשֶּׁ֒מֶשׁ֒ וְשָׁכַ֣ב²⁷ בְּשַׂלְמָת֖וֹ וּבֵֽרֲכֶ֑ךָ וּלְךָ֙

תִּהְיֶ֣ה צְדָקָ֔ה לִפְנֵ֖י יְהוָ֥ה אֱלֹהֶֽיךָ׃ ס

14 לֹא־תַעֲשֹׁ֥ק שָׂכִ֖יר עָנִ֣י וְאֶבְי֑וֹן מֵאַחֶ֕יךָ א֧וֹ מִגֵּרְךָ֛ אֲשֶׁ֥ר בְּאַרְצְךָ֖ בִּשְׁעָרֶֽיךָ׃

15 בְּיוֹמוֹ֩ תִתֵּ֨ן שְׂכָר֜וֹ וְֽלֹא־תָב֧וֹא עָלָ֣יו הַשֶּׁ֗מֶשׁ כִּ֤י עָנִי֙ ה֔וּא²⁸ וְאֵלָ֕יו ה֖וּא נֹשֵׂ֥א

---

²⁶ Typically, when the infinitive construct with כְּ precedes a clause, the כְּ is construed temporally ("when. . ."), and when it follows the clause, it is construed correlatively ("as . . ."). However, fixed phrases such as this are the exception to that tendency, and they can be located either before or after the phrase they modify. The sun in the Bible is said to "enter" in the evening and to "come out" in the morning.

²⁷ Based on the flow of the passage, what modality would you assign to this converted perfect?

²⁸ Is this verbless clause identifying or descriptive? How do you know? (See section 15.8.)

אֶת־נַפְשׁוֹ[29] וְלֹא־יִקָּרֵא עָלֶיךָ[30] אֶל־יְהֹוָה וְהָיָה בְךָ[31] חֵטְא: ס

16    לֹא־יוּמְתוּ אָבוֹת עַל־בָּנִים וּבָנִים לֹא־יוּמְתוּ עַל־אָבוֹת אִישׁ[32] בְּחֶטְאוֹ

יוּמָתוּ: ס

17    לֹא תַטֶּה[33] מִשְׁפַּט גֵּר יָתוֹם וְלֹא תַחֲבֹל בֶּגֶד אַלְמָנָה:

---

[29] The phrase וְאֵלָיו . . . אֶת־נַפְשׁוֹ is at least somewhat idioimatic. What English phrase would be the equivalent?

[30] What use of עַל is this? (See *IBHS* section 11.2.13.)

[31] What use of בְ is this? (See *IBHS* section 11.2.5.)

[32] Note that this noun is singular and that the following verb is plural. This is a distributive use of אִישׁ, meaning "each man."

[33] This is a third doubly weak verb in this passage.

18   וְזָכַרְתָּ֗ כִּ֣י עֶ֤בֶד הָיִ֙יתָ֙ בְּמִצְרַ֔יִם וַֽיִּפְדְּךָ֛ יְהוָ֥ה אֱלֹהֶ֖יךָ מִשָּׁ֑ם עַל־כֵּ֞ן אָנֹכִ֤י

מְצַוְּךָ֙ לַעֲשׂ֔וֹת אֶת־הַדָּבָ֖ר הַזֶּֽה׃ ס

# PART III

## Readings in the Psalms

The Psalms help you begin to gain experience reading Hebrew poetry. Poetry generally has a looser set of syntactical constraints. What it loses in precision, however, it often gains in emotional power. Hebrew poetry tends to omit many particles, such as the definite direct object marker, prepositions, the definite article, etc. It also tends to gap words, especially in the second colon of a bicolon. As you work through these three psalms, beware of "translational inertia," as the Masoretic Text may not say exactly what you expect based on your memory of English translations.

**23** [1] מִזְמֹ֥ור לְדָוִ֑ד[1] יְהוָ֥ה רֹ֝עִ֗י לֹ֣א אֶחְסָֽר׃

2 בִּנְאֹ֣ות דֶּ֭שֶׁא יַרְבִּיצֵ֑נִי[2] עַל־מֵ֖י מְנֻחֹ֣ות[3] יְנַהֲלֵֽנִי׃

---

[1] Note that the function of the ל in לְדָוִד is worth careful consideration. The phrase is typically translated "of David," but you should examine an intermediate syntax and determine "Of David in what sense?" Is this the *lamed auctoris* or another use of ל? (See *IBHS* section 11.2.10.)

[2] Is this verb Qal or Hiphil? How does that impact the nuance and the metaphor that is developing over the first three verses of the psalm?

[3] What genitive relationship is indicated by this construct phrase? (See *IBHS* section 9.5.3.) Notice that the more sparing nature of poetry–fewer words–leads to more possibilities in understanding various syntactical relationships.

3 נַפְשִׁ֥י[4] יְשׁוֹבֵ֑ב[5] יַֽנְחֵ֥נִי בְמַעְגְּלֵי־צֶ֝֗דֶק לְמַ֣עַן שְׁמֽוֹ׃

4 גַּ֤ם[6] כִּֽי־[7]אֵלֵ֨ךְ בְּגֵ֪יא צַלְמָ֡וֶת[8] לֹא־אִ֘ירָ֤א רָ֗ע כִּי־[9]אַתָּ֥ה עִמָּדִ֑י שִׁבְטְךָ֥

וּ֝מִשְׁעַנְתֶּ֗ךָ הֵ֣מָּה יְנַחֲמֻֽנִי׃

---

[4] With נֶ֫פֶשׁ be careful not to impart a more Greek "soul vs. body" distinction, but to recognize the semantic range of the term in Hebrew.

[5] This form is typically parsed as a Polel (the doubling stem for a hollow root). What is the root, and how would you translate the form? (See section 28.6.)

[6] The typical gloss "also" is probably insufficient here. What other glosses of גַּם might be more appropriate in this context?

[7] Which use of כִּי is represented here? (See section 14.10.)

[8] Consider the traditional translation "shadow of death" comes from a supposed etymology of צֵל + מָ֫וֶת. This is more likely a more concrete image from a steep-sided Ancient Near Eastern wadi. Check a lexicon for the gloss for this term. How does it connect with the imagery of sheep and shepherd?

[9] Which use of כִּי is represented here? (See section 14.10.)

5    תַּעֲרֹ֤ךְ לְפָנַ֨י ׀ שֻׁלְחָ֗ן נֶ֥גֶד צֹרְרָ֑י[10] דִּשַּׁ֖נְתָּ[11] בַשֶּׁ֥מֶן רֹאשִׁ֗י כּוֹסִ֥י רְוָיָֽה׃

6    אַ֤ךְ ׀ ט֤וֹב וָחֶ֣סֶד[12] יִ֭רְדְּפוּנִי כָּל־יְמֵ֣י חַיָּ֑י וְשַׁבְתִּ֥י[13] בְּבֵית־יְהֹוָ֗ה לְאֹ֣רֶךְ יָמִֽים׃

---

[10] Is this word singular or plural? How do you know? Note that the vowel has been lengthened because this is a pausal form. (See sections 11.3 and 13.5.)

[11] This verb is typically glossed "anoint," but note that it is *not* a kingly anointing. What word would be used for a kingly anointing? What is the semantic range of דשׁן and what is its usage here? If necessary, consult a lexicon for the range of uses to which שֶׁמֶן was put. Also compare the parsing of this verb to that of the first verb in this verse. The change in tenses would require a different translation in prose; however, in poetry it often seems that tenses are used indiscriminately. Grammarians debate whether the perfect versus imperfect distinction is meaningful in poetry and, if it is, what it implies.

[12] Remember the challenge of glossing a word as multifaceted as חֶסֶד.

[13] Do not let "translational inertia" overcome you here. Parse this verb. What is its root as given here in the Masoretic Text? How would that be translated? Now check the BHS text critical note. What is the Septuagint reading, and how would the Hebrew text need to be pointed to explain that reading? What part of speech would that require this word to be? What reading is implied by the Syriac? What Hebrew root would produce that reading? Look at the parallelism of this verse. Which reading do you find most likely authentic and why?

**24** 1 לְדָוִד מִזְמוֹר לַיהוָה[14] הָאָרֶץ וּמְלוֹאָהּ תֵּבֵל[15] וְיֹשְׁבֵי[16] בָהּ[17]׃

2 כִּי[18]־הוּא עַל־יַמִּים יְסָדָהּ וְעַל־נְהָרוֹת יְכוֹנְנֶהָ[19]׃

3 מִי־יַעֲלֶה בְהַר־יְהוָה וּמִי־יָקוּם בִּמְקוֹם קָדְשׁוֹ[20]׃

---

[14] Which use of ל is this? (See section 11.5.) The expression of possession does not require the use of יֵשׁ.

[15] Check your lexicon. What is the semantic range of this word in contrast to that of אֶרֶץ, with which it is parallel? What is the parallelism between the two cola of this verse? (See section 10.10.)

[16] This is a participle in the construct form. Remember that participles are verbal nouns, which means they can take both absolute and construct forms as well as being singular and plural. (See sections 9.5 and 10.3.)

[17] Note the instance of gapping here, which is common in Hebrew poetry. (See section 26.10.) What is gapped from the first portion of the verse?

[18] Which use of כִּי is represented here? Do not let the start of a new verse overly influence your decision, but look at the context of the poem. (See section 14.10.)

[19] This is another common Polel form. What is the root, and how would you translate the form? (See section 28.6.) Note again that the typical translational values for various tenses are much more varied in poetry, with its relaxed syntactic requirements. This form contextually needs to be translated in the past tense.

[20] Note carefully the pronunciation of the first vowel, which indicates the original qotl form of this noun. (See section 10.3.)

4     נְקִ֣י[21] כַפַּ֗יִם וּֽבַר־לֵ֫בָ֥ב אֲשֶׁ֤ר ׀ לֹא־נָשָׂ֣א לַשָּׁ֣וְא[22] נַפְשִׁ֑י[23] וְלֹ֖א נִשְׁבַּ֣ע

לְמִרְמָֽה׃

5     יִשָּׂ֣א[24] בְרָכָ֣ה מֵאֵ֣ת יְהוָ֑ה וּ֝צְדָקָ֗ה[25] מֵאֱלֹהֵ֥י יִשְׁעֽוֹ׃[26]

---

[21] Your translation will need to include "The one with" in advance of your translation of these construct phrases.

[22] What is the semantic range of שָׁוְא, and what is its use in context here? (See sections 5.7 and 6.7.) Is the poet only thinking of dishonesty, or is he equating dishonesty and idolatry? Alternately, is this a reference to Exodus 20 and taking God's name in vain? The challenge of poetry, with its lack of precision, is that a case can often be made for more than one reading.

[23] As the Masoretic Text has this form, how would you have to translate it? Check the BHS text critical note. How would it suggest reading this word? What letter confusion could cause this difference? How likely do you think it is that these variants arose from letter confusion? (See section 2.11.) Note also the possibility that–unlike what is typical in prose–the poet means to invoke more than a single meaning of the word.

[24] Here used a bit idiomatically; the gloss is "receive."

[25] The verb that governs this noun has again been gapped.

[26] The addition of the suffixed pronoun has caused the word to resyllabize and therefore revocalize. (See section 11.3.)

6     זֶה[27] דּ֣וֹר דֹּרְשָׁ֑ו[28] מְבַקְשֵׁ֨י פָנֶ֖יךָ[29] יַעֲקֹ֣ב[30] סֶֽלָה׃

7     שְׂא֤וּ[31] שְׁעָרִ֨ים׀[32] רָאשֵׁיכֶ֗ם וְֽ֭הִנָּשְׂאוּ פִּתְחֵ֣י עוֹלָ֑ם[33] וְ֝יָב֗וֹא[34] מֶ֣לֶךְ הַכָּבֽוֹד׃

8     מִ֥י זֶה֮[35] מֶ֤לֶךְ הַכָּ֫ב֥וֹד יְהוָה֮ עִזּ֪וּז וְגִבּ֥וֹר יְהוָ֗ה גִּבּ֥וֹר מִלְחָמָֽה׃

---

[27] Consult a research lexicon. What glosses other than the simple demonstrative "this" might make more contextual sense for this use of זֶה?

[28] If you have trouble with this form, see sections 8.12 and 11.3.

[29] The sudden switch to a second person pronoun is not unusual in the Psalms.

[30] This word is a conundrum for interpreters. One could follow the Septuagint reading, which also has τοῦ θεοῦ. (See the BHS text critical note.) Alternately, one could read יַעֲקֹב as a vocative ("O Jacob"), or יַעֲקֹב could be read as appositional to מְבַקְשֵׁי פָנֶיךָ.

[31] Note how many times this root has been used in the psalm. It seems in some sense to be a keyword for this poem.

[32] This is a vocative form—"o gates."

[33] What genitive relationship does this construct form indicate? (See *IBHS* section 9.5.3.)

[34] Note the parsing of the verbs that precede this one. How should this verb therefore be translated? (See section 25.7.) This feature would be more apparent in prose, but it has been used by the poet here.

[35] This is not simply the demonstrative, but is a particular use of זֶה, used to stress the question, expressing almost exasperation in a question, similar to saying the English idiom "who *in the world* . . . ?"

9     שְׂא֤וּ שְׁעָרִ֨ים ׀ רָאשֵׁיכֶ֗ם וּשְׂאוּ[36] פִּתְחֵ֣י עוֹלָ֑ם וְיָבֹא מֶ֣לֶךְ הַכָּבֽוֹד׃

10     מִ֤י ה֣וּא זֶה֮ מֶ֤לֶךְ הַכָּב֥וֹד יְהוָ֣ה צְבָא֑וֹת ה֤וּא מֶ֣לֶךְ הַכָּב֣וֹד סֶֽלָה׃[37]

---

[36] Compare to verse 7 and then consider the BHS text critical note. What do you believe represents the original reading of this word and why?

[37] Which word in this verse has been added in comparison to verse 8? How does it even further stress the question?

**100** ¹ מִזְמֹ֥ור לְתֹודָ֑ה³⁸ הָרִ֥יעוּ לַ֝יהוָ֗ה כָּל־הָאָֽרֶץ׃

² עִבְד֣וּ אֶת־יְהוָ֣ה בְּשִׂמְחָ֑ה בֹּ֥אוּ לְ֝פָנָ֗יו בִּרְנָנָֽה׃

³ דְּע֗וּ כִּֽי³⁹־יְהוָה֮ ה֤וּא אֱלֹ֫הִ֥ים הֽוּא־עָ֭שָׂנוּ וְלֹ֣א⁴⁰ אֲנַ֑חְנוּ עַ֝מֹּ֗ו וְצֹ֣אן מַרְעִיתֹֽו׃⁴¹

⁴ בֹּ֤אוּ שְׁעָרָ֨יו ׀ בְּתֹודָ֗ה חֲצֵרֹתָ֥יו בִּתְהִלָּ֑ה הֹֽודוּ⁴²־לֹ֝֗ו בָּרֲכ֥וּ שְׁמֹֽו׃⁴³

---

³⁸ Which portion of the semantic range of תּוֹדָה is intended here? How do you make that judgment?

³⁹ Note that כִּי follows the verb ידע. What use of is this? (See section 14.10.)

⁴⁰ Note carefully the impact of this Ketiv/Qere! What would the change in the meaning of the verse be? (See section 8.12.)

⁴¹ Note that the poem moves from a typical bicolon form to a tricolon form, where each line of poetry naturally divides into 3 sections.

⁴² This is a doubly weak verb. How is it parsed? (See section 24.2.)

⁴³ This verse is most commonly read as a tricolon but could be read as containing two separate parallelisms in an ABAB pattern. Which do you prefer and why?

5    כִּי־טֹ֣וב יְ֭הוָה לְעֹולָ֣ם חַסְדֹּ֑ו וְעַד־דֹּ֥ר וָדֹר֮[44] אֱמוּנָתֹֽו׃

---

[44] This is an idiomatic construction meaning "to all generations."

Psalm 19 gives you practice with a more challenging Hebrew poem.  Much of the challenge of Psalm 19 comes from its terseness, leading to the interpretive challenge of how to understand the metaphor that dominates its first half.  Also pay particular attention to Psalm 19 as an example of parallelism.  (See sections 10.10 and 26.10.)

1     לַמְנַצֵּחַ[1] מִזְמוֹר לְדָוִד׃[2]

2     הַשָּׁמַיִם מְסַפְּרִים כְּבוֹד־אֵל[3] וּמַעֲשֵׂה יָדָיו מַגִּיד[4] הָרָקִיעַ׃[5]

---

[1] The final vowel is the furtive *pataḥ*.  (See section 5.4.)

[2] Note that the superscription to the psalm, which is not given a verse number in English translations, is verse 1 in the Hebrew text.  The Hebrew and English versification of any psalm with a verse-length superscription will therefore differ by one.

[3] What portion of the semantic range of כָּבוֹד is indicated here?  (See section 6.7.c.)

[4] This exemplifies the figurative language of poetry.  The שָׁמַיִם and רָקִיעַ do not verbally "speak," but they do "declare."  How do you understand this metaphor?

[5] Note the word pair שָׁמַיִם and רָקִיעַ.  These types of word pairs are quite standard in poetry, especially in bicola.  They have been argued to be evidence of standard pairs that were taught, though further research has pointed out that pairs like this can be independently generated by a word association game.

3      יֹום לְיֹום יַבִּיעַ אֹמֶר וְלַיְלָה לְּלַיְלָה[6] יְחַוֶּה[7]־דָּעַת׃

4      אֵין־אֹמֶר וְאֵין דְּבָרִים בְּלִי[8] נִשְׁמָע קֹולָם׃[9]

5      בְּכָל־הָאָרֶץ ׀ יָצָא קַוָּם[10] וּבִקְצֵה תֵבֵל[11] מִלֵּיהֶם לַשֶּׁמֶשׁ שָׂם־אֹהֶל בָּהֶם׃

---

[6] Note the anomalous dagesh in the first ל.

[7] Note that the ו is consonantal, as it has a *segol* vowel. How does this cause you to interpret the remainder of the Masoretic markings? This verb is often simply glossed "express." Check your lexicon. Is there a more specific nuance you can give in translation?

[8] בְּלִי can be a particle of negation in poetry (e.g., Is. 32:10; Hos. 8:7, 9:16; Job 41:18), not simply glossed as "without" (e.g., Deut. 4:42; Jer. 2:15; etc.) There are two diametrically opposed ways to therefore understand this verse. How would you understand it if you gloss בְּלִי as "not"? How would you understand it if you gloss בְּלִי as "without"? The challenge in deciding between these two possible interpretations is the terseness of the line of poetry, which leaves both interpretations possible.

[9] Note that the antecedent for this object pronoun must be from verse 2. Why?

[10] Note again the vowel marker on the ו, indicating it is a consonant. This is therefore not a verbal form. Check your lexicon. What is the typical gloss for קַו? Because this gloss does not seem to fit well with the line, many interpreters look to the parallelism (מִלֵּיהֶם). Consult the *HALOT* lexical entry on קַו. Isaiah 28 has a use of the word which seems to fit that parallelism. Alternately, *HALOT*'s entry also notes the proposal that the text was originally קֹולָם and the ל was lost due to a copyist error. Also consult the text critical note in BHS regarding the Septuagint's reading of this verse. What do you feel the correct reading would be for this word and why? How would you translate it?

[11] Check your lexicon. What is the semantic range of this word in contrast to that of אֶרֶץ, with which it is parallel?

6  וְה֤וּא[12] כְּחָתָ֗ן יֹצֵ֪א מֵחֻפָּ֫ת֥וֹ יָשִׂ֥ישׂ כְּגִבּ֗וֹר לָר֥וּץ אֹֽרַח׃

7  מִקְצֵ֤ה הַשָּׁמַ֨יִם ׀ מֽוֹצָא֗וֹ[13] וּתְקוּפָת֥וֹ עַל־קְצוֹתָ֑ם[14] וְאֵ֥ין נִ֝סְתָּ֗ר מֵֽחַמָּתֽוֹ׃

8  תּ֘וֹרַ֤ת יְהוָ֣ה תְּ֭מִימָה[15] מְשִׁ֣יבַת[16] נָ֑פֶשׁ[17] עֵד֥וּת יְהוָ֥ה נֶ֝אֱמָנָ֗ה מַחְכִּ֥ימַת

פֶּֽתִי׃[18]

---

[12] The antecedent of הוּא is שֶׁמֶשׁ from the previous verse. The sun is being personified as a חָתָן. יָצָא means rising when used with the sun in an Ancient Near Eastern context, as the sun is understood to be "going out" from its sleeping place.

[13] First translate these three words with a formal translation philosophy. Then use a more dynamic translation philosophy to render their meaning in English. (See section 21.7.)

[14] What is the nearest masculine plural noun that would therefore be the natural antecedent of the possessive pronoun that is suffixed to this noun?

[15] Note that verbless clause word order rules (see section 15.8) are not applicable in poetry, as it has relaxed syntactic constraints. This is a descriptive clause, even though the subject precedes the predicate. It would be ungrammatical in prose, but in poetry this word order for a descriptive clause is acceptable.

[16] Note that this is a participle which has then been placed in the construct form to become part of a construct phrase. (See section 10.2.)

[17] This phrase sets the pattern for this section of the poem, where Torah (or a synonym) is described by an adjective and then described by the effect it has on a person.

[18] What gloss will you choose for פֶּתִי? Check a research lexicon and do a small word study on this term. What nuances do you need to understand for the term to correctly explain it?

9    פִּקּוּדֵי יְהוָה יְשָׁרִים מְשַׂמְּחֵי־לֵב מִצְוַת יְהוָה בָּרָה[19] מְאִירַת עֵינָיִם׃

10    יִרְאַת יְהוָה טְהוֹרָה עוֹמֶדֶת[20] לָעַד מִשְׁפְּטֵי־יְהוָה אֱמֶת צָדְקוּ יַחְדָּו׃

11    הַנֶּחֱמָדִים[21] מִזָּהָב[22] וּמִפַּז רָב וּמְתוּקִים מִדְּבַשׁ וְנֹפֶת צוּפִים׃[23]

12    גַּם־עַבְדְּךָ נִזְהָר[24] בָּהֶם[25] בְּשָׁמְרָם[26] עֵקֶב רָב׃

---

[19] The ESV and RSV gloss this word as "pure," whereas the NIV glosses it as "radiant." Look up the word in your lexicon. Check the other uses of this word in the Old Testament/Hebrew Bible. How would each translation justify its choice of gloss? Which do you prefer and why?

[20] Note that the pattern breaks here, as this participle is in the absolute, not construct, form. How can you tell the difference?

[21] The challenge of this participle is determining its referent. What is the closest masculine plural noun with which it could agree? Alternately, it could be referencing the entire list of synonyms for Torah.

[22] What use of מִן is this? (See section 9.6.)

[23] Having translated the first portion (vv. 1–6) and second (vv. 7–11) of the poem, how do these two sections correspond?

[24] Note the final vowel of this verb, which will help you distinguish between a perfect verbal form and a participle. (See section 19.5.)

[25] What use of בְ is this? (See *IBHS* section 11.2.5.)

[26] Is the suffix subjective or objective? How do you know? (See section 13.3.)

13    שְׁגִיאֹות[27] מִי־יָבִין מִנִּסְתָּרֹות נַקֵּנִי[28]׃

14    גַּם מִזֵּדִים[29] חֲשֹׂךְ עַבְדֶּךָ אַל־יִמְשְׁלוּ־בִי אָז אֵיתָם[30] וְנִקֵּיתִי[31] מִפֶּשַׁע רָב׃

15    יִהְיוּ לְרָצֹון[32] אִמְרֵי־פִי וְהֶגְיֹון לִבִּי לְפָנֶיךָ יְהוָה צוּרִי וְגֹאֲלִי[33]׃

---

[27] Consult the Masoretic marginal notation in the Masorah Parva. What does it indicate? Check a lexicon for the gloss for this word. In what two ways has that gloss been determined? (See sections 18.6, 22.9, and 23.6.)

[28] Note that this is a Piel form of נקה used with מִן. Check your lexicon and use these two factors to determine the portion of the semantic range of נקה that you should use as you translate this verse.

[29] What is the semantic range of this term in comparison to שְׁגִיאֹות and נִסְתָּרֹות in the previous verse? Consult the BHS text critical note on this word. According to the note, what would a retroversion of the Septuagint text into Hebrew give? What letter confusion could have produced the two variant readings? (See section 2.11.) Which reading do you think is more likely authentic and why?

[30] This is from a geminate root. How do you parse it?

[31] The vowel pointing could be parsed as either a Piel or a Niphal form. Given the use of the preposition מִן, which is more likely?

[32] Which portion of the semantic range of רָצֹון is most appropriate here? Why? (See sections 5.7 and 6.7.)

[33] Now having translated the third portion (v.12-15) of the poem, how does it correspond to the first two sections?

# PART IV

Readings in Prophetic Literature

Micah 6:1–8 and Amos 2:1–5 provide a first reading in the prophetic literature.  The Hebrew prophets utilized a range of literary forms, with Micah 6:1-8 involving the common literary form of a covenant lawsuit.  Note the common elements such as the calling of witnesses, the rehearsal of God's goodness, the accusation, and the sentencing.  Amos 2:1–5 gives an example of two short judgment oracles.  Note the parallels between them and particularly the parallels with what precedes and follows this section of the book of Amos.

M6:1 שִׁמְעוּ־נָ֕א [1] אֵ֥ת אֲשֶׁר־יְהוָ֖ה אֹמֵ֑ר [2] ק֚וּם רִ֣יב אֶת־ [3] הֶ֣הָרִ֔ים וְתִשְׁמַ֖עְנָה [4]

הַגְּבָע֖וֹת קוֹלֶֽךָ׃

2    שִׁמְע֤וּ הָרִים֙ [5] אֶת־רִ֣יב יְהוָ֔ה וְהָאֵתָנִ֖ים [6] מֹ֣סְדֵי אָ֑רֶץ כִּ֣י רִ֤יב לַֽיהוָה֙ [7] עִם־

---

[1] What is the function of this particle?  (See section 8.8.)

[2] What time sense (tense) should you use to translate this predicative participle?  Why?  (See section 9.5.)

[3] This is an atypical use of אֵת to mean, assuming the Masoretic Text is correct, "before."

[4] This could formally be either an imperfect or a jussive form.  Which is it and why?  (See section 7.4.)

[5] Given the parsing of the preceding verb, which use of the nominative function is this?  (See *IBHS* section 8.3.)

[6] The BHS text critical note would emend this form to be a verb.  What is its nominal translation, and what would be the translation of the form proposed in BHS?

[7] What use of ל is this?  (See section 11.5.)

עַמּוֹ וְעִם־יִשְׂרָאֵל יִתְוַכָּח׃

3    עַמִּי מֶה־עָשִׂיתִי לְךָ וּמָה הֶלְאֵתִיךָ עֲנֵה בִי׃[8]

4    כִּי הֶעֱלִתִיךָ מֵאֶרֶץ מִצְרַיִם וּמִבֵּית עֲבָדִים פְּדִיתִיךָ וָאֶשְׁלַח לְפָנֶיךָ אֶת־

מֹשֶׁה אַהֲרֹן וּמִרְיָם׃

5    עַמִּי[9] זְכָר־נָא מַה־יָּעַץ בָּלָק מֶלֶךְ מוֹאָב וּמֶה־עָנָה אֹתוֹ בִּלְעָם בֶּן־בְּעוֹר

_____

[8] Consult a research lexicon.  What is the proper gloss for ענה when it governs its object with בְּ?

[9] What does the BHS text critical note propose for this word?  If you were to accept that suggestion, how would your translation change?

מִן־הַשִּׁטִּים֙ עַד־הַגִּלְגָּ֔ל לְמַ֕עַן דַּ֖עַת צִדְק֥וֹת יְהוָֽה׃

6    בַּמָּה֙ אֲקַדֵּ֣ם יְהוָ֔ה אִכַּף֙[10] לֵאלֹהֵ֣י מָר֑וֹם הַאֲקַדְּמֶ֣נּוּ בְעוֹל֔וֹת בַּעֲגָלִ֖ים בְּנֵ֥י

שָׁנָֽה׃

7    הֲיִרְצֶ֤ה יְהוָה֙ בְּאַלְפֵ֣י אֵילִ֔ים בְּרִֽבְב֖וֹת נַֽחֲלֵי־שָׁ֑מֶן[11] הַאֶתֵּ֤ן[12] בְּכוֹרִי֙ פִּשְׁעִ֔י

פְּרִ֥י בִטְנִ֖י חַטַּ֥את נַפְשִֽׁי׃

---

[10] This is a geminate verb.  (See section 28.3.)  Be guided by the consonantal prefix more than the vowel.

[11] What explains the unusual vocalization of this word?  (See section 13.5.)

[12] After נתן each of the following pairs of nouns is considered to be in exchange for the other.

8   הִגִּ֥יד לְךָ֛ אָדָ֖ם¹³ מַה־טּ֑וֹב וּמָֽה־יְהוָ֞ה דּוֹרֵ֣שׁ מִמְּךָ֗ כִּ֣י אִם־¹⁴עֲשׂ֤וֹת מִשְׁפָּט֙

וְאַ֣הֲבַת חֶ֔סֶד וְהַצְנֵ֥עַ¹⁵ לֶ֖כֶת עִם־אֱלֹהֶֽיךָ׃¹⁶ פ

---

¹³ Given the preceding pronoun, which use of the nominative function is this?  (See *IBHS* section 8.3.)

¹⁴ Read the collocation כִּי אִם together.  How are these words glossed?

¹⁵ Consult *HALOT* for a discussion of the difficulty of translation of this word.

¹⁶ Note that typical English translations make this verse appear to contain three commands, but there are two infinitive constructs that structure this command.  מִשְׁפָּט and אַהֲבַת חֶסֶד are therefore paired.  Based on a lexical analysis of each term, how do they fit together?

A2:1 כֹּה אָמַ֣ר יְהֹוָ֗ה עַל־שְׁלֹשָׁה֙ פִּשְׁעֵ֣י מוֹאָ֔ב וְעַל־אַרְבָּעָ֖ה לֹ֣א אֲשִׁיבֶ֑נּוּ עַל־

שָׂרְפ֛וֹ[17] עַצְמ֥וֹת מֶֽלֶךְ־אֱד֖וֹם לַשִּֽׂיד׃

2 וְשִׁלַּחְתִּי[18]־אֵ֣שׁ בְּמוֹאָ֔ב[19] וְאָכְלָ֖ה אַרְמְנ֣וֹת הַקְּרִיּ֑וֹת וּמֵ֤ת בְּשָׁאוֹן֙ מוֹאָ֔ב

בִּתְרוּעָ֖ה[20] בְּק֥וֹל שׁוֹפָֽר׃

3 וְהִכְרַתִּ֥י שׁוֹפֵ֖ט מִקִּרְבָּ֑הּ וְכָל־שָׂרֶ֛יהָ אֶהֱר֥וֹג עִמּ֖וֹ אָמַ֥ר[21] יְהֹוָֽה׃ פ

---

[17] Parse this word carefully. Let the correct pronunciation guide you. (See section 2.5.)

[18] What is the sense of the ו in connection with verse 1?

[19] What use of בְּ is this? (See *IBHS* section 11.2.5.)

[20] Is this the same use of בְּ or different? How do you know? (See *IBHS* section 11.2.5.)

[21] What use of the perfect is this? (See *IBHS* section 30.5.)

4  כֹּה אָמַר יְהוָה עַל־שְׁלֹשָׁהֹ פִּשְׁעֵי יְהוּדָה וְעַל־אַרְבָּעָה לֹא אֲשִׁיבֶנּוּ עַל־

מָאֳסָם[22] אֶת־תּוֹרַת יְהוָה[23] וְחֻקָּיוֹ לֹא שָׁמָרוּ וַיַּתְעוּם[24] כִּזְבֵיהֶם[25] אֲשֶׁר־

הָלְכוּ אֲבוֹתָם אַחֲרֵיהֶם:[26]

5  וְשִׁלַּחְתִּי אֵשׁ בִּיהוּדָה וְאָכְלָה אַרְמְנוֹת יְרוּשָׁלָ͏ִם:[27] פ

---

[22] Note the parallel structure to verse 1.  What parsing should you therefore expect for this word?

[23] Given the parallels between the oracles, note also the difference.  How do the crimes enunciated for Judah differ from those enunciated in the preceding oracle?

[24] Note that the sequence in this narrative form is not temporal, as it would be in prose, but is instead a logical sequence.

[25] Is this the subject or the object of the verb?  How do you know?

[26] Note the resumptive pronoun.  What is its antecedent?  (See section 11.4.)

[27] Note the parallels between this oracle and the one that preceded it.  Consult an English translation and compare this to the oracles in chapter 1 and to the oracle that follows in the remainder of chapter 2.  Given Amos's role as a prophet to the northern kingdom of Israel, what is the rhetorical function of this parallel structure?

Isaiah 53, the second example of prophetic literature, is one of the famous "servant songs" of the second portion of the book of Isaiah. This will be a challenging passage to translate, with several verses where major translations give different interpretations of the Hebrew. (Consult them only **after** you have translated the passage yourself to the best of your ability.) Pay particular attention to dividing the verses into poetic lines–the use of bicola to structure the song and think carefully through the possible relationships between the various words in each colon. (See section 26.10.) Note also the large number of words employed by the prophet in the semantic range of affliction and suffering.

13 הִנֵּה יַשְׂכִּיל[1] עַבְדִּי יָרוּם וְנִשָּׂא וְגָבַה מְאֹד׃

14 כַּאֲשֶׁר שָׁמְמוּ עָלֶיךָ[2] רַבִּים כֵּן־מִשְׁחַת מֵאִישׁ[3] מַרְאֵהוּ וְתֹאֲרוֹ מִבְּנֵי אָדָם׃

---

[1] Is there any significance to the fact that a Hiphil form of this root is used here (instead of Qal, Piel, etc.)? (See section 20.10.) There are two distinct, though clearly related, pieces of the semantic range of this root. Which one do you contextually choose here and why? (See sections 5.7 and 6.7.)

[2] Some translations follow the MT in translation, while others accept the recommendation of the BHS apparatus. What are the two options, and which do you prefer? Why?

[3] This word seemingly interrupts a construct phrase. Translate it separately and then determine how it fits with the surrounding words. What use of מִן is this? (See section 9.6.)

15 כֵּן יַזֶּה⁴ גּוֹיִם רַבִּים עָלָיו יִקְפְּצוּ מְלָכִים פִּיהֶם כִּי אֲשֶׁר לֹא־סֻפַּר לָהֶם

רָאוּ וַאֲשֶׁר לֹא־שָׁמְעוּ הִתְבּוֹנָנוּ:⁵

1 מִי הֶאֱמִין לִשְׁמֻעָתֵנוּ⁶ וּזְרוֹעַ יְהוָה עַל־מִי נִגְלָתָה:

2 וַיַּעַל כַּיּוֹנֵק לְפָנָיו וְכַשֹּׁרֶשׁ מֵאֶרֶץ צִיָּה לֹא־תֹאַר לוֹ וְלֹא הָדָר⁷ וְנִרְאֵהוּ

---

⁴ Only the second root letter of this verb is visible in this inflected form. What possibilities exist to explain the loss of the first and third root letters? How do you parse this verb? The BHS critical apparatus provides several other suggestions for emendation. What are they? Do you prefer any of them, and if so, why?

⁵ Notice the form that clearly resembles a Hithpael but has a different vowel pattern. What type of verbal roots typically cause this type of form? (See section 28.6.)

⁶ Among the various major English translations this is translated as "what we have heard" (NRSV, HCSB, and NJPS), "our message" (NIV), and "what he has heard from us" (ESV, but with "what we have heard" noted as an alternative translation). Based on lexical and syntactic work, which do you feel most accurately reflects this phrase and why?

⁷ Most translations do not treat the athnach as indicating the parallelism here. How do you structure this verse? How many bicola are there and how do you justify your division of the words into various cola? (See section 26.10.)

וְלֹא־מַרְאֶ֖ה וְנֶחְמְדֵֽהוּ׃

3    נִבְזֶה֙ וַחֲדַ֣ל אִישִׁ֔ים[8] אִ֥ישׁ מַכְאֹב֖וֹת וִיד֣וּעַ[9] חֹ֑לִי וּכְמַסְתֵּ֤ר[10] פָּנִים֙ מִמֶּ֔נּוּ[11]

נִבְזֶ֖ה וְלֹ֥א חֲשַׁבְנֻֽהוּ׃

4    אָכֵ֤ן חֳלָיֵ֙נוּ֙ ה֣וּא נָשָׂ֔א וּמַכְאֹבֵ֖ינוּ סְבָלָ֑ם וַאֲנַ֣חְנוּ חֲשַׁבְנֻ֔הוּ נָג֛וּעַ מֻכֵּ֥ה[12]

---

[8] What genitive relationship is indicated by this construct phrase? (See *IBHS* section 9.5.)

[9] Note from the BHS apparatus that many ancient witnesses imply a revocalization would be appropriate here. (See section 16.10.)

[10] As vocalized, this is a noun, but the evidence of the Isaiah manuscript from the Dead Sea Scrolls suggests revocalizing it as a Hiphil participle. What would that vocalization be? (See section 16.10.)

[11] מִמֶּ֔נּוּ is מִן plus either a 3ms or 1cp suffix. (The forms are identical–see section 11.2.) The three-word phrase וּכְמַסְתֵּ֤ר פָּנִים֙ מִמֶּ֔נּוּ could therefore be translated two ways based on this preposition and suffix. What are the two options?

[12] Only one letter from the verbal root is visible in this participle form. What is the root, and how is this form parsed? (See section 24.7.)

אֱלֹהִים[13] וּמְעֻנֶּה׃

5 וְהוּא מְחֹלָל מִפְּשָׁעֵנוּ[14] מְדֻכָּא מֵעֲוֺנֹתֵינוּ מוּסַר שְׁלוֹמֵנוּ עָלָיו וּבַחֲבֻרָתוֹ

נִרְפָּא־לָנוּ׃

6 כֻּלָּנוּ[15] כַּצֹּאן תָּעִינוּ אִישׁ לְדַרְכּוֹ פָּנִינוּ וַיהוָה הִפְגִּיעַ בּוֹ אֵת עֲוֺן כֻּלָּנוּ׃

7 נִגַּשׂ וְהוּא נַעֲנֶה וְלֹא יִפְתַּח־פִּיו כַּשֶּׂה לַטֶּבַח יוּבָל וּכְרָחֵל לִפְנֵי גֹזְזֶיהָ

---

[13] Is this noun meant to be the subject of both participles or just the first? In prose, it would seem to be grouped with the first participle, but in poetry either is possible.

[14] What use of מִן is this? (See *IBHS* section 11.2.11.)

[15] If you have trouble recognizing this word, remove the possessive suffix and then remember that o-class and u-class vowels are related. (See section 1.3.)

נֶאֱלָ֔מָה וְלֹ֥א יִפְתַּ֖ח פִּֽיו׃

8 מֵעֹ֤צֶר וּמִמִּשְׁפָּט֙[16] לֻקָּ֔ח וְאֶת־דּוֹר֖וֹ מִ֣י יְשׂוֹחֵ֑חַ[17] כִּ֤י[18] נִגְזַר֙ מֵאֶ֣רֶץ חַיִּ֔ים

מִפֶּ֥שַׁע עַמִּ֖י נֶ֥גַע לָֽמוֹ׃[19]

9 וַיִּתֵּ֤ן אֶת־רְשָׁעִים֙ קִבְר֔וֹ וְאֶת־עָשִׁ֖יר בְּמֹתָ֑יו עַ֚ל לֹא־חָמָ֣ס עָשָׂ֔ה וְלֹ֥א מִרְמָ֖ה

בְּפִֽיו׃

---

[16] Return to your lexical analysis of this word from Micah 6:8. What portion of the semantic range is intended here? How do you know? (See section 6.7.)

[17] This form is typically parsed as a Polel of the root שׂיח. Consult a research lexicon. What major interpretations of this form of the verb are proposed?

[18] How you translate the previous four words will largely determine how you understand this form of כִּי. (See section 14.10.)

[19] This is an alternate form of the preposition לְ plus the pronominal suffix.

10     וַיהוָ֞ה חָפֵ֤ץ דַּכְּאוֹ֙²⁰ הֶֽחֱלִ֔י אִם־תָּשִׂ֤ים²¹ אָשָׁם֙ נַפְשׁ֔וֹ יִרְאֶ֥ה זֶ֖רַע²² יַאֲרִ֣יךְ

יָמִ֑ים וְחֵ֥פֶץ יְהוָ֖ה בְּיָד֥וֹ יִצְלָֽח׃

11     מֵעֲמַ֤ל נַפְשׁוֹ֙ יִרְאֶ֣ה²³ יִשְׂבָּ֔ע בְּדַעְתּ֗וֹ יַצְדִּ֥יק צַדִּ֛יק עַבְדִּ֖י לָֽרַבִּ֑ים וַעֲוֹֽנֹתָ֖ם

הֻ֥וא יִסְבֹּֽל׃

---

[20] Is this suffix subjective or objective? How do you know? (See section 13.3.)

[21] This verb could be parsed two different ways, yielding two different subjects. What are they? How would that change your translation and understanding of the verse?

[22] An emendation is often proposed to yield the reading "his arm" (meaning "his vindication"). What emendation would be required to create this reading? (See section 16.10.)

[23] This Isaiah scroll in the Dead Sea Scrolls also has "light," which is reflected in some English translations (e.g., NIV).

12    לָכֵ֞ן אֲחַלֶּק־ל֣וֹ בָרַבִּ֗ים²⁵ וְאֶת־עֲצוּמִים֮ יְחַלֵּ֣ק שָׁלָל֒ תַּ֗חַת אֲשֶׁ֨ר הֶעֱרָ֤ה²⁴

לַמָּ֙וֶת֙ נַפְשׁ֔וֹ וְאֶת־פֹּשְׁעִ֖ים נִמְנָ֑ה וְהוּא֙ חֵטְא־רַבִּ֣ים נָשָׂ֔א וְלַפֹּשְׁעִ֖ים

ס ²⁶יַפְגִּֽיעַ׃

---

²⁴ This is often glossed into English as "divide." Based on the lexical entry for חלק, what sense does that gloss mean to imply?

²⁵ This could be glossed as "great" or "many." Which do you prefer and why?

²⁶ Note the two very different glosses in the semantic range for this root in both the Qal and the Hiphil.

91

# PART V

---

## Readings in Wisdom Literature

Proverbs by nature are terse sayings, possibly the tersest of all Hebrew literature, providing an apt challenge for your developing skill in reading Hebrew poetry.  Sections of the book of Proverbs from chapters 10 to 30 show little immediately apparent organization, with each proverb having to be interpreted independently.  Pay particular attention to the parallelism and the relationship between the A and the B cola in each proverb.  Proverbs also can have multiple layers of meaning, including taking advantage of double entendre or multiple meanings of words.  Proverbs 28:1-16 will also provide you with a thorough review of participles (see chapter 9) and some of the major uses of בְּ (see *IBHS* section 11.2.5).

1 נָ֨סוּ֙[1] וְאֵין־רֹדֵ֣ף רָשָׁ֔ע וְצַדִּיקִ֖ים[2] כִּכְפִ֣יר יִבְטָֽח׃

2 בְּפֶ֣שַֽׁע אֶ֭רֶץ[3] רַבִּ֣ים שָׂרֶ֑יהָ וּבְאָדָ֥ם[4] מֵבִ֥ין יֹדֵ֗עַ כֵּ֣ן יַאֲרִֽיךְ׃

---

[1] The BHS text critical note suggests reading this as a singular verb to agree with the subject.  How does it explain the presence of what it views as an extra ו in the text?  (See section 28.9.)

[2] Remember that ו is fundamentally a connecting particle, and do not slavishly translate it with "and."  What is the correct gloss for ו in this context?  The BHS apparatus suggests also reading this substantive as a singular form.  How do you assess this suggestion?

[3] What genitive function is expressed by this construct phrase?  (See *IBHS* section 9.5.1.)

[4] The two participles that follow are serving as attributive adjectives.  (See section 9.5.)

3 גֶּבֶר רָשׁ וְעֹשֵׁק דַּלִּים מָטָר סֹחֵף וְאֵין לָחֶם:[5]

4 עֹזְבֵי[6] תוֹרָה יְהַלְלוּ רָשָׁע וְשֹׁמְרֵי תוֹרָה יִתְגָּרוּ[7] בָם[8]: פ

5 אַנְשֵׁי־רָע לֹא־יָבִינוּ מִשְׁפָּט וּמְבַקְשֵׁי יְהוָה יָבִינוּ כֹל:

6 טוֹב־רָשׁ הוֹלֵךְ בְּתֻמּוֹ מֵעִקֵּשׁ[9] דְּרָכַיִם וְהוּא עָשִׁיר:

7 נוֹצֵר תּוֹרָה בֵּן מֵבִין וְרֹעֶה זוֹלְלִים יַכְלִים אָבִיו:

---

[5] What is the relationship between the two halves of this verse?
[6] What use of the participle is this? (See section 9.5.)
[7] Is this a dagesh lene or dagesh forte? How do you know? (See section 2.1.)
[8] What use of בְּ is this? (See *IBHS* section 11.2.5.)
[9] What use of מִן is this? (See section 9.6.)

8 מַרְבֶּ֣ה ה֭וֹנוֹ בְּנֶ֣שֶׁךְ וּבְתַרְבִּ֑ית[10] לְחוֹנֵ֖ן דַּלִּ֣ים יִקְבְּצֶֽנּוּ׃

9 מֵסִ֣יר אָ֭זְנוֹ מִשְּׁמֹ֣עַ תּוֹרָ֑ה גַּֽם־תְּ֝פִלָּת֗וֹ תּוֹעֵבָֽה׃

10 מַשְׁגֶּ֤ה יְשָׁרִ֨ים ׀ בְּדֶ֥רֶךְ רָ֗ע בִּשְׁחוּת֥וֹ הֽוּא־יִפּ֑וֹל וּ֝תְמִימִ֗ים יִנְחֲלוּ־טֽוֹב׃

11 חָכָ֣ם בְּ֭עֵינָיו אִ֣ישׁ עָשִׁ֑יר וְדַ֖ל מֵבִ֣ין יַחְקְרֶֽנּוּ׃

12 בַּעֲלֹ֣ץ[11] צַ֭דִּיקִים רַבָּ֣ה תִפְאָ֑רֶת וּבְק֥וּם רְ֝שָׁעִ֗ים יְחֻפַּ֥שׂ[12] אָדָֽם׃

---

[10] Note the Qetiv/Qere here. The BHS text critical note suggests this word should be deleted. Why? (See section 28.9.)

[11] What use of בַ is this? (See *IBHS* section 11.2.5.)

[12] In light of the Septuagint, how does the BHS apparatus suggest reading this word? How would that change your parsing and translation?

13 מְכַסֶּה פְשָׁעָיו לֹא יַצְלִיחַ וּמוֹדֶה וְעֹזֵב יְרֻחָם׃

14 אַשְׁרֵי אָדָם מְפַחֵד תָּמִיד וּמַקְשֶׁה לִבּוֹ יִפּוֹל בְּרָעָה׃

15 אֲרִי־נֹהֵם וְדֹב שׁוֹקֵק מֹשֵׁל רָשָׁע עַל עַם־דָּל׃

16 נָגִיד חֲסַר תְּבוּנוֹת וְרַב[13] מַעֲשַׁקּוֹת שֹׂנֵאי[14] בֶצַע יַאֲרִיךְ יָמִים׃ פ

---

[13] Note from the BHS text critical apparatus that many of the ancient versions omit the ו. Doing so would make this verse into a bicolon, with all the text before the athnach being the A colon. Consult also the text critical note on the word שֹׂנֵאי. How might the ו have been accidentally moved by a copyist of this verse? If you accept that reading, how would you translate the first half of the verse? What would the opposition then be between the A and the B cola of the poetic line?

[14] Note another Qetiv/Qere. How does the Qere differ in parsing from the Qetiv?

Job 28 is a poem about wisdom, one that gives wisdom but also takes wisdom to read.  A major challenge of Job as a book, which is true of chapter 28 as well, is the difficulty of its vocabulary, with a very high proportion of loanwords and hapax legomena.  (See sections 22.9 and 23.6.)  The ambiguity of the vocabulary makes the interpretation of the metaphors in this poem particularly challenging.  Do not settle for the metaphor apparent in the English translation of your choice, but instead consider other possible glosses for each term and how those alternate glosses might change the controlling metaphor of the poem.

1  כִּי[1] יֵשׁ לַכֶּסֶף מוֹצָא וּמָקוֹם לַזָּהָב יָזֹקּוּ:[2]

2  בַּרְזֶל מֵעָפָר יֻקָּח[3] וְאֶבֶן[4] יָצוּק[5] נְחוּשָׁה:

---

[1] What use of כִּי is this?  How do you justify your choice?  (See section 14.10.)

[2] Let the dagesh help you parse this form.  (See section 28.3.)  In considering your choice of gloss for this form, compare this verse with both Isaiah 28:18 and Malachi 3:3.

[3] Based on the Masoretic vowel pointing, how should this form be parsed?  What parsing might be preferred? (See section 17.8.)

[4] Note that the preposition from the first half of the verse has been gapped from before this word.  (See section 26.10.)

[5] How would this be parsed as currently written and pointed?  (There are two possibilities.)  See the BHS note for a suggested emendation.  How would the BHS emendation be parsed?  Which do you think is more likely to be the original reading?  Why?

3     קֵ֤ץ ׀ שָׂ֨ם[6] לַחֹ֗שֶׁךְ וּֽלְכָל־תַּ֭כְלִית ה֣וּא חוֹקֵ֑ר אֶ֖בֶן אֹ֣פֶל וְצַלְמָֽוֶת[7]׃

4     פָּ֤רַץ נַ֨חַל ׀ מֵֽעִם־גָּר[8] הַֽנִּשְׁכָּחִ֥ים מִנִּי[9]־רָ֑גֶל דַּ֖לּוּ מֵאֱנ֣וֹשׁ[10] נָֽעוּ[11]׃

5     אֶ֗רֶץ מִמֶּ֥נָּה יֵֽצֵא־לָ֑חֶם וְ֝תַחְתֶּ֗יהָ נֶהְפַּ֥ךְ[12] כְּמוֹ־אֵֽשׁ׃

---

[6] Part of the challenge of interpreting the controlling metaphor of the first eleven verses is the subject of this 3ms verb. What are the various options you could validly use for the subject, and how does each of them change how you might gloss the vocabulary of the passage and therefore understand the metaphor of this verse and of the whole section?

[7] See the note on Psalm 23:4.

[8] How would the proposed emendation in the BHS text critical note be read? Which do you prefer and why?

[9] This is a variant "long form" of מִן.

[10] What use of מִן is this? (See *IBHS* section 11.2.11.)

[11] The usual gloss of "tremble" does not work well contextually. What other glosses are suggested in a more advanced lexicon?

[12] Note the use of the Niphal of this root in Jonah 3:4. Note the parsing of this form. The pronouns on the two prepositions are feminine singular, indicating that אֶרֶץ is treated as feminine in this verse, so what is the subject of this verb?

100

6    מְקוֹם־סַפִּיר[13] אֲבָנֶיהָ וְעַפְרֹת זָהָב לוֹ:[14]

7    נָתִיב לֹא־יְדָעוֹ עָיִט וְלֹא שְׁזָפַתּוּ עֵין אַיָּה:

8    לֹא־הִדְרִיכֻהוּ בְנֵי־שָׁחַץ[15] לֹא־עָדָה עָלָיו שָׁחַל:[16]

9    בַּחַלָּמִישׁ שָׁלַח יָדוֹ הָפַךְ מִשֹּׁרֶשׁ הָרִים:

---

[13] Do not be confused by the English cognate. What is the correct gloss, and how does it differ from "sapphire"?

[14] Note how this pronoun complicates the masculine versus feminine agreement in the poem. It makes one suspect that the parallelism is driving the change of gender in the pronoun.

[15] This word only occurs in the Hebrew Bible in collocation with בְנֵי. Based on the gloss in your lexicon, what type of genitive relationship is the phrase? (See *IBHS* section 9.5.)

[16] This is typically glossed as "lion," though there are other proposals. Consult *HALOT*. What is the support in cognate languages for "lion" as the correct gloss? (See sections 22.9 and 23.6.)

10   בַּצּוּרוֹת יְאֹרִים[17] בִּקֵּעַ וְכָל־יְקָר רָאֲתָה עֵינֽוֹ׃

11   מִבְּכִי[18] נְהָרוֹת חִבֵּשׁ וְתַעֲלֻמָהּ[19] יֹצִא אֽוֹר[20]׃ פ[21]

12   וְהַחָכְמָה[22] מֵאַיִן תִּמָּצֵא וְאֵי זֶה[23] מְקוֹם בִּינָֽה׃

---

[17] יְאֹרִים is the plural form of יְאֹר, the Nile. In the plural, it references the Nile delta, where the river forms many branches. If the traditional understanding of the controlling analogy of mining holds, these are considered to be flooded channels in the mine.

[18] How would you translate this as pointed? *HALOT* proposes a revocalization of this word. What would the revocalization produce as a translation? (See section 16.10.)

[19] For the mappiq, note the text critical note in BHS.

[20] Note again the tendency of Hebrew poetry to drop prepositions and particles. (See section 26.10.) What preposition should you supply before this word? Parse the preceding verb carefully to help you make this decision.

[21] Based on your translation and analysis, summarize the basic point the poet is making in the first eleven verses of the poem.

[22] This use of the definite article is to mark a concept. (See *IBHS* section 13.5.g.)

[23] See the note on Psalm 24:8.

13    לֹא־יָדַע אֱנוֹשׁ עֶרְכָּהּ²⁴ וְלֹא תִמָּצֵא בְּאֶרֶץ הַחַיִּים׃

14    תְּהוֹם אָמַר לֹא בִי־הִיא וְיָם²⁵ אָמַר אֵין עִמָּדִי׃

15    לֹא־יֻתַּן²⁶ סְגוֹר²⁷ תַּחְתֶּיהָ וְלֹא יִשָּׁקֵל כֶּסֶף מְחִירָהּ׃

16    לֹא־תְסֻלֶּה²⁸ בְּכֶתֶם אוֹפִיר²⁹ בְּשֹׁהַם יָקָר וְסַפִּיר׃

---

²⁴ This could work contextually, but it does seem somewhat odd. Consult the BHS text critical note. How would the Septuagint translation be retroverted into Hebrew? Which reading do you believe is most likely the original reading and why?

²⁵ What is the relationship between תְּהוֹם and יָם in this parallelism?

²⁶ Is this a Pual or a Qal passive? (See section 17.8.)

²⁷ Consider revocalizing this word. What options might contextually be preferable to סְגוֹר? (See section 16.10.)

²⁸ How is this parsed? Note that it seems to be a byform of the root סלא.

²⁹ What type of genitive relationship is indicated by this construct phrase? (See *IBHS* section 9.5.)

17 לֹא־יַעַרְכֶנָּה[30] זָהָב וּזְכוֹכִית וּתְמוּרָתָהּ כְּלִי־פָז:

18 רָאמוֹת וְגָבִישׁ לֹא יִזָּכֵר[31] וּמֶשֶׁךְ חָכְמָה מִפְּנִינִים:[32]

19 לֹא־יַעַרְכֶנָּה פִּטְדַת־כּוּשׁ בְּכֶתֶם טָהוֹר לֹא תְסֻלֶּה: פ[33]

20 וְהַחָכְמָה מֵאַיִן תָּבוֹא[34] וְאֵי זֶה מְקוֹם בִּינָה:

---

[30] This is a somewhat idiomatic use of the root, glossed as "to be equal."

[31] Do not too quickly gloss זכר as remember. What other glosses are possible? What modality contextually fits best for this imperfect form? (See section 5.2.)

[32] Lamentations 4:7 indicates that this is red, sometimes leading to a translation as "rubies." What other gloss is possible? What use of מִן is this? (See section 9.6.)

[33] Now summarize the point of verses 12-19. How does this relate to the point of verses 1-11?

[34] Notice the slight change in emphasis compared to verse 12.

21 וְנֶעֶלְמָה מֵעֵינֵי כָל־חָי וּמֵעוֹף הַשָּׁמַיִם נִסְתָּרָה׃

22 אֲבַדּוֹן וָמָוֶת אָמְרוּ[35] בְּאָזְנֵינוּ שָׁמַעְנוּ שִׁמְעָהּ׃[36]

23 אֱלֹהִים הֵבִין דַּרְכָּהּ[37] וְהוּא יָדַע אֶת־מְקוֹמָהּ׃

24 כִּי־הוּא[38] לִקְצוֹת־הָאָרֶץ יַבִּיט תַּחַת כָּל־הַשָּׁמַיִם יִרְאֶה׃

25 לַעֲשׂוֹת לָרוּחַ מִשְׁקָל וּמַיִם תִּכֵּן בְּמִדָּה׃[39]

---

[35] It is often argued that this phrasing indicates second-hand knowledge.
[36] Now summarize the point of verses 20-22. How does this relate to the first two sections of the poem?
[37] Check the BHS text critical note. Which reading do you consider most likely original and why?
[38] What use of כְ is this? How do you justify your choice? (See section 14.10.)
[39] Note the similarities between this imagery and Job 38 as well as Proverbs 8.

26     בַּעֲשֹׂתוֹ[40] לַמָּטָר חֹק וְדֶרֶךְ לַחֲזִיז קֹלוֹת׃

27     אָז רָאָה וַיְסַפְּרָהּ[41] הֱכִינָהּ וְגַם־חֲקָרָהּ׃

28     וַיֹּאמֶר לָאָדָם הֵן יִרְאַת אֲדֹנָי הִיא חָכְמָה וְסוּר מֵרָע בִּינָה׃ ס[42]

---

[40] What use of בְּ with the infinitive construct is this? (See section 13.2.)

[41] Which gloss of ספר fits best contextually?

[42] Finally, summarize the point of verses 23-28. How does it relate to the point of the first three sections of the poem? What is the thought movement of the poem from beginning to end? Many interpreters want to detach this final verse from the remainder of the poem, but note that it is a fairly standard feature of wisdom literature (e.g., Ecclesiastes 12:13–14).